One From
the Road

Peter Sampson

RoperPenberthy Publishing Ltd

Published by RoperPenberthy Publishing Ltd,
Springfield House,
23 OatlandsDrive,
Weybridge,
Surrey
KT13 9LZ

ISBN 978-1-903905-77-2

Typeset by **documen**, www.documen.co.uk
Printed in the United Kingdom by Knowledgepoint, Reading

CONTENTS

Prologue

"Whereabouts unknown". These words became familiar to me each week as I queued with my mother waiting to be interviewed by the National Assistance Officer.

This was a ritual that kept us from destitution while we lodged with my grandparents during a time when we did not know whether or not my father would eventually return home.

It had seemed a long time since Mother travelled to Scotland with Grandma Maggie and had found that Father had discharged himself from the Infirmary in Carstairs to which he had been sent whilst still serving with the 1st Battalion, Oxfordshire and Buckinghamshire Light Infantry after returning, injured, to England from the North West European theatre of war.

I was sometimes asked by my peers at school as to where my father was now and did not like to explain that his whereabouts was unknown, so I satisfied them with a statement that he had not returned from the war. Most of my friends, therefore, assumed that he was dead as a number of them were now fatherless too. This state of affairs lasted from 1946 till about 1956, when, having left school and started a course of study at Technical College I received a letter from my father asking me to meet him in Kentish Town.

I had never been to London alone before and my family were not keen on me making any such rendezvous. I was therefore dissuaded from finding him especially as his infrequent visits to his home town of Maidstone were met with severe disapproval by his own parents.

I had gleaned over the years that he was most likely a vagrant and that his mental state precluded him from taking regular employment.

I still had a longing to seek him out and let him know that at least he had a son that cared for him, but this desire remained dormant until after I was married and had a family of my own.

It was not until ten years of marriage had passed that I determined to find him. This was because of our new birth as Christians when a dramatic change took place in our lives as Iris, my dear wife, and I were awakened by the call of the Gospel and in that very hour God spoke through His Holy Spirit and compelled us to seek one who was afar off.

The only means available to us in our search were to write to several agencies who may have had contact with my vagrant father through the post war years.

Or was this so? We now had access to an all seeing and all knowing God through prayer. We determined to pray night and morning for three weeks for the resolution of the matter.

Three weeks to the day my father sat in our lounge at home at Burham, near Rochester, in his home county of Kent. This was the beginning of a huge change in our family life and whilst we were glad to accommodate this erstwhile vagrant we had no concept of the awful consequences that were to follow from our hospitality.

Father had previously been free to roam as he pleased, except whilst detained in Her Majesty's penal institutions, and clearly did not intend to settle down so soon! We had to learn to deal with a heretofore unexpected reality and proved over the next decade the power of prayer every time that Father disappeared from home.

This book is a testimony to the kindness of many friends during this harrowing period of our lives as we endeavoured to raise two young children who became devoted to their Grandad. But more than that, it is to the glory of God that we were able to continue and finish the commission that He had set us at the time of our conversion.

The story is sometimes outrageously funny and at other times pathetically sad as it follows us through three homes during which time we prayed for and saw the reunion of Mother and Father, their departure into Glory and the disdain that some poured out on the final chapter of Pop's life.

There is no bitterness remaining, however; just the knowledge that we have done the Lord's bidding in His time.

Peter Sampson

Introduction

An unhappy childhood, including a motorcycle accident involving the death of his friend, a time living in Canada, a career in the Army, a short courtship and marriage to my Mother.

These few phrases sum up my father's life before the time this book introduces the reader to a world that is unknown to most, and pieces together the years of separation from a father that I longed for when a child and whose burden I was commissioned to shoulder as a man.

This is a story that could not be told were it not for the reality of answered prayer from a faithful and merciful God whose direction we were compelled to follow in faith.

The drama began for my wife Iris and I in 1972 following our conversion through the Holy Spirit when we were directed through the Scriptures to find a man who has been a vagrant for twenty eight years. The changes wrought in our lives as we repatriated him and sought to reunite him with the wife he once loved are spelled out together with all the sadness, joy and humour this work involved.

My father's life during the second world war has been thoroughly researched. I have stood on the spot at the edge of a field in Normandy where his Bren gun carrier was destroyed and have followed the route of his unit from

Arromanches to Falaise from where he was returned to England, a broken man.

The accounts of his years of vagrancy are derived from the stories he told us during his more lucid days while I have my own memories of the period when he lived with us in Kent and Sussex.

Foreword

Introducing a book regarding the life of my grandfather
– a character who I did not meet until I was seven – is an
unusual task.

Kenneth Ewart Sampson, or "Pop" as he became known,
was one of thousands of soldiers whose lives were altered
irrevocably by the traumas of military engagement during
the Second World War.

What makes my grandfather's story unusual, if not
unique, was the way in which he was"found" to be reunited,
firstly with his son's family, then with his wife, and then
with his brother and sister and their respective families. For
nearly twenty-eight years – from 1945 to 1972 – it had been
accepted that my grandfather had vanished, or "run-away"
as I was told in simple terms, when as a six year old, I had
worked out that I had two maternal grandparents and only
one paternal grandparent and wanted to know why.

It had been accepted by his siblings that he was one of the
thousands who simply never survived the Second World War,
that he was no longer alive. My father believed that he was
and the story of his discovery and subsequent reunification
with his family, is one that is in parts both moving and
very funny. It is a tale that is entwined with my father's
unshakeable faith and religious beliefs. Among more secular

relatives and friends it is still a remarkable tale and one that my father wishes to record for posterity.

My own memories of my grandfather began on 1st July 1972, when, returning to our home in the village of Burham, Kent, from a morning spent shopping in nearby Maidstone with my mother Iris and my sister Beverley, there was a strange man in the kitchen who had rotten teeth and continually muttered to himself. I was taken upstairs and it was explained to me that the strange man was in fact my grandfather.

There would be many traumas and incidents to come in the years ahead but from an early age I was fond of my granddad. He was kind to us as children and he was kind to animals. He also had a good sense of humour. His habit of mumbling sentiments that most adults, faced with the same situation, dare not say, was a source of great amusement to me as a child.

Over the years my father showed great strength of character and unshakeable faith in what he believed was his mission to reunite his disparate family, and this book serves as a record and testament to his remarkable achievement in so doing.

Mark Sampson
February 2011.

Acknowledgements

It would not have been possible to publish this biography of my father without the help interest and understanding of the friends, acquaintances and historians who have both known and tolerated him and have understood his foibles.

Firstly our dear friends, John and Lois Underdown and their family, together with the Pastor and congregation of Enon Baptist Chapel, Chatham, between 1972 and 1975.

The people in Burham who knew Pop, especially the landlords of the public houses and our once nearest neighbours, Derek and Ruth Linkens who we visited in Sheffield.

Our wider relations, cousins and their wives who readily accepted him as part of our family.

"The Epic of Malta" published by Odhams Press.

"Fortress Malta" by James Holland.

The staff at the Royal Greenjackets Museum in Winchester.

The Royal West Kent Museum, Maidstone.

John H. Roberts, Hon. Sec., 43rd Light Infantry Old Comrades.

Pastor of Zoar Chapel, The Dicker, J.W. Sperling-Tyler FRAS.

Coleridge and Rhett Comber, owners of the Yew Tree Chalvington at that time and many of their clientele.

Staff of Harebeating nursing home, Hailsham.

M Xavier Leroy et son famille vers Falaise, Normandie, France.

My paternal cousins Michael Sampson and Adrian Jenner and their wives who have made subsequent family concord possible.

Together with all those kind enough to tolerate my father from time to time when we met with them, either socially, in chapels or in the streets.

1 *Gun Wharf*

IIIIIIIIIIIIIIIIIIIIIIIIIIIIIIIIIIIIIIIIIIIIIIIIIIIIIIIIIIIIIIIIIIIIIIIIIIIIIIIIIIIIIIIIIIIIIIIIIIIIIIIIIIIIIIIIIIIIIIIIIIIIIIIIIIII

It was unusual to see, on that warm summer night, a police car drive slowly around the park-like walks newly created on the site of the old gun wharf fronting the river at Chatham. The Medway glistened and long reflections pointed, finger-like, towards John and me from the lights of ships moored around the reach. We sat in the shadows watching.

It was past midnight. Headlights picked out a row of benches close to the riverside and the car stopped. Two policemen got out and removed from the back seat a human form, which they sat between them on a nearby bench." A drunk", murmured John." Yes, I suppose it's better than a night in the cells though", I replied. We fell silent as the car withdrew and soon the only sound was the straining of the securing chains attached to the nearby mooring buoys as the rising tide pushed relentlessly inland.

Soon the dark figure in front of us lay down oblivious of his surroundings and I commented quietly that somewhere my father was probably in a similar state and I hoped that he too would be treated as mercifully as those two Kent policemen had treated the vagrant before us. "Have you no idea what has happened to your old man?" asked John.

I soon found myself whispering to my companion and voicing my thoughts aloud about the man I had only seen once and whose whereabouts were as elusive as the log we had watched, half an hour earlier, bobbing its way upstream on the rising tide from the estuary.

John and I often visited Chatham or Gillingham at night time, sometimes after an evening in a country hostelry. We would settle our stomachs with a steaming hot pie purchased from the stall on the forecourt of Chatham Station or from a "chippie" in The Brook and then, like this evening,walk slowly onto the Gun Wharf. The atmosphere of this place grips me still, with the remains of narrow gauge railway lines still visible crossing the footways, which bring to mind the small but heavy hand-propelled bogies, perhaps loaded with cannon, being trundled along by barefoot sailors loading a man-of-war moored at the wharf.

Now, however, the lights reflecting in the water quickly changed from the oil-lit ports of clinker-built warships, in our imagination, to the cold electric glow of a small container ship as the harsh realities of the seventies seized us.

There in front of us was the form of a human being, unaware of his surroundings and at this moment nobody wanted him. Even the Police had found him sufficiently uninteresting that they had simply set him down to dry out. Would he face a similar day tomorrow – here or somewhere else? Who would care? Who would want to know? Every encounter would receive another rebuff.

We did not understand the plight of this man and I wondered what had become of those who he once cared for. What sort of people could they be to have become so careless of him?

I looked down at my well-soled shoes as the answers to these questions suddenly struck me. I knew deep down that sometime, somewhere, I would have to face the reality and shoulder the responsibility of finding out about a man in similar circumstances. I would have to face knowledge that I would very much prefer not to know. After all, life had been reasonably well-ordered until now.

With love from Kenneth & Marjorie

2 *My Father*

Kenneth Ewart Sampson was born on 14th November 1910 at No 2, Melville Road, Maidstone, the county town of Kent. His father and mother were both teachers at two of the town's well established church-sponsored elementary schools nearby, St. Philip's and All Saints. They were shortly to move into larger accommodation in St. Philip's Avenue to house their growing family." Ginger" Sampson, as grandfather John was known to his pupils, was a great disciplinarian and his young son often knew the pain of a severe beating. Indeed, a neighbour told my mother that following such punishment Ken was often sent into the cellar for the night so his cries would not be heard by the neighbours. His sister Marjorie told me that, "he squealed like a pig" when his father hit him with a belt.

"Pop" as he later became affectionately known, thought that he was disowned by his father because he failed the scholarship examination which would have given him a coveted place at the Grammar School, where his brother Eric and I later attended. Instead my Dad had a technical school education which was hugely beneath the aspirations of his ambitious and proud parents.

When Father was about twelve years old he found himself the proud owner of a dog, bought for him as a present. He always showed affection to animals and this remained a notable characteristic in his later life. His father, however, was not amused when the dog was disrespectful of the floor indoors and he took my dad, with his dog, out into their back garden and shot the dog, an incident he never forgot.

Father's early working days were spent initially as an invoice clerk at Sharp's "Kreemy Toffee" works in St. Peter's Street, but later, during 1927 and 1928, he was to be found in the offices of the nearby factory of Messrs. Tilling-Stevens Ltd., who manufactured commercial vehicle chassis. This seemed a more fitting role for a lad who had had a technical education and he later put this experience to good use when he lived in Canada.

One summer in the late 1920s while his mother and father went for a holiday to Margate, Ken looked at a gleaming motor cycle in the rear garden of their home and, though inexperienced as a rider, suggested to his friend, the postman's son, that they should go for a spin on his father's bike. This joy-ride finished in disaster; they hit a car at a notorious road junction near the "Chiltern Hundreds" public house on the Sittingbourne Road.

These were the days before crash-helmets. His friend was killed instantly and Ken was concussed for two weeks, during which time he lay in hospital. Grandfather was incensed as he had to cut short his holiday and had lost his prized motorbike, now a useless wreck.

This unhappy period of Ken's life was partially brought to an end when he was sent to stay with Uncle Frank Brown and Aunt Emma at their bungalow in Well Street, Loose, near Maidstone, but the distance from home was apparently not far enough away from his parents and his father soon suggested that he should go to live in Canada, at Ingersoll, Ontario, with his Uncle George.

The ignominy of having a son who not only mixed with the postman's son, but who had the indignity of having the story of how he had killed him printed in the Kent Messenger, was too much for this smug man who felt superior to his fellows and had become ashamed of his eldest boy.

Early in the 1950s Uncle George made a visit to England and Mother and I met him at the bungalow at Loose. At the end of the evening he walked us to "The Bird in Hand" at Coxheath to catch the bus home. There was a few inches of snow on the ground, the sky was bright with stars and it was freezing. Uncle George said it reminded him of times around Ingersoll when he had gone walking with my father. I felt that I now had an understanding of what life must have been like for my Dad in those days, the weather adding to the reality of the tales. We were told of how Ken, while living in Canada, would travel to work at the Ford Motor Works at Detroit every day.

The Canadians –
Uncle George from Ingersoll and Uncle Frank from Loose

I once saw my father at close quarters when I was a child. This was during the severe winter of 1947 and I remember going with him to a barber's shop in Boxley Road opposite the grey walls of the prison. I walked with him from the bus stop beside the "Royal George" ending up with wet feet due to the slushy snow, my eight-year-old legs being too short to step over the melt heaped up at the roadside. I remember, though, the security of holding my Dad's hand as we walked on the smooth ice. This relationship was to be short lived, however, as grandfather Jack didn't want him to be seen in the town again and he left before making any attempt to settle down.

Father joined the army in Maidstone on his return from Canada in 1931, but later transferred to a Yorkshire Regiment, the Green Howards, rather than continue with the local militia at their depot in Maidstone where his military career had begun. He now clearly felt more comfortable away from his parents.

Mother told me that she had visited him at Catterick Camp following their wedding for a short leave before his posting to Malta and humorously said that the train journey to Yorkshire must have kindled an embryonic interest in railways in me as she had been forced to stand for six hours from King's Cross before arriving at Richmond!

In my early school years I was frequently at home with poor health suffering with numerous chest problems and on one occasion I was sitting in a warm bed watching large snowflakes amassing in the corners of the window panes.

Now and then the wind would blow some away, only to be replaced by others sliding down the glass. I remember asking Mother what people without a home would do to keep warm outside. She did not answer. Whilst still at school I heard once again from my father when he visited Maidstone, calling at our home to leave a Christmas present, "The Boys' Book of Modern Marvels" which I treasured for a long time. On this occasion Mother made several attempts to locate him but found that he had not returned to the Church Army hostel where he had spent the previous night and had not been recorded at either of the common lodging houses in Stone Street that week. I remember well my disgust at the squalor and stench inside these establishments as I went there with my Mother and tried to find my Dad. The smell of cooking cabbage, stale fat and urine are indelibly etched on my mind We subsequently found that Ken had visited Aunt Emma and Uncle Frank at their home at Loose and had spent one night in their chicken shed because he had been living rough and was "lousy".

When questioned by my peers about my Dad I usually said that he had not come home from the war. I felt ashamed knowing that this was a half truth but it was readily accepted as a number of my classmates had lost their fathers during the war years.

As I grew into adulthood I put the plight of my father to the back of my mind.

Pop's birthplace – 2, Melville Road, Maidstone

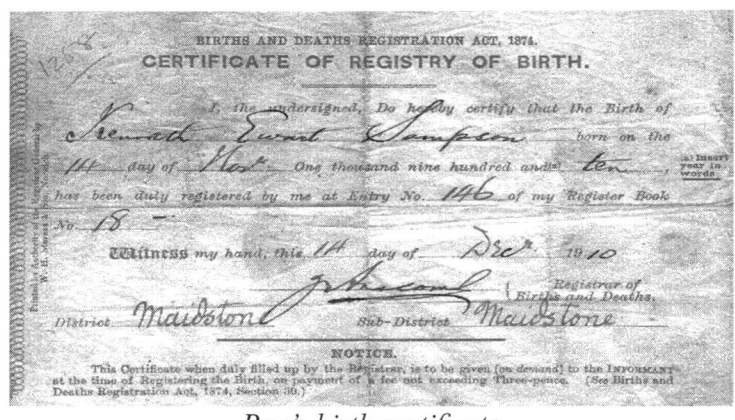

Pop's birth certificate

3 *A Child's View*

Married life for my Mother lasted little more than the four days of their honeymoon taken at the Imperial Hotel, Sheerness during May 1938. My father had been known to the family for some time as an army friend of my mother's older brother, my uncle Henry.

The depot of the Royal West Kent Regiment was in Maidstone and my maternal grandparents' home was known for its warmth and hospitality both before and during the years of the Second World War. It was not unknown for uncle Henry to arrive, unannounced, at home with some of his pals from the barracks, including my future father, Ken, to raid the larder and then to spend a convivial evening in company of his brother Fred and sisters Betty, Lottie and Lucy, who was later to become my mother.

6341658 Kenneth Ewart Sampson was often one of those to be entertained at home and, despite his traumatic war experiences and the events that followed, he always remembered his Service Number. Although Ken and Lucy had become friends, I think it came as a bit of a surprise to both families when they announced they were to be married, by special licence, a few days before Ken rejoined the Green Howard Regiment on 16th May 1938 at Catterick, Yorks.

Ken was posted to Malta during July of that year and, except for five months duty in Palestine – during which time I was born – he remained in the island fortress until the siege was over and the brave people of that island had been awarded the George Cross.

I was born on 16th February 1939 while Mother was still living with her parents and as war was declared on 3rd September there was clearly little hope of us having our own home and so it transpired that my childhood and youth were spent in a loving and secure home with my Mother, her parents and her two younger sisters Betty and Lottie, both of whom I saw married from their parental home.

Aunt Lottie had been a Jewish Czech refugee, whom my grandparents took in and later adopted. We subsequently learned that her parents had died during the holocaust – most likely at Auschwitz via the Terezin ghetto. Lieselotte last saw her mother one morning at Prague Station where she became one of Nicolas Winton's 669 rescued children of "the lost generation". Her mother told her that she was going for a summer holiday!

I had become very fond of her being only a baby when she first came into our home and she, as a twelve year old, naturally poured out her affection on me, sometimes taking me for walks in my pram. Later I was told of an occasion in 1941 when she had lain across my pram to protect me from a marauding German plane that was strafing along the road where she was pushing me.

The war held no fear for me although it was very real despite my tender years. Our home in Sandling Lane was opposite the sports fields of the Invicta Lines, then home to the 13th Infantry Training Corps and strategically placed on the sandstone ridge north of Maidstone where we had a good view of aircraft flying from the fighter stations at Detling and West Malling.

Our back lawn provided plenty of space for a toddler who watched many dog-fights and saw planes fall burning from the sky. I also witnessed our own Spitfires and Hurricanes tip over "doodle-bugs", or V1 flying-bombs, with their wing tips and send them to earth or back in the direction from whence they came.

My most vivid memory from those years was the morning just preceding D-Day when the sky was darkened by literally thousands of bombers – American, British and Canadian – as they flew low over the housetops for seemingly hours on end. The only explanation forthcoming from the adults that morning was that "this is it". The planes returned higher and in looser formation by evening, but without news of any invasion yet.

We were used to the clatter of the tracks from Bren gun carriers and light tanks but imagine my surprise to find our lane completely blocked one morning with American tanks. I was reprimanded by Grandad later in the day for trading our daily newspapers for bars of chewing gum. I thought I had a bargain! This was early June 1944 and I had no idea that not many miles away my own father was being prepared to cross the channel as part of an army to reinforce troops now fighting fiercely the Nazi aggressor on French soil.

Towards the end of the war, mother realised that the chance of father returning home to a settled way of life were unlikely. It was then that she decided to foster and later adopt a new baby brother for me, and so Michael Oliver appeared on the scene. A lovely, curly haired child to whom I became fond in those early years of my life.

Doodle-bugs appeared in the skies of Kent during 1945 and we would listen intently for them until the throb of their engines stopped. In the ensuing silence we would dive for cover, under a table or into the Morrison shelter in our dining room.

One night, before dawn, and whilst half asleep, we became conscious of an eerie silence. Then came the deep thud of a V1 hitting the ground with the explosion following soon after. Michael was found, still asleep in his cot, his head being the only part visible. The mercy of God had protected him from a plaster ceiling that had entirely collapsed over his cot. Mother and I later went to see the crash-site near the sheep-wash, off Grange lane, and I remember the charred trees and the water-filled crater that remained there for years after.

These were the idyllic pre-school years!

Mother and Father's wedding party – Sanding Lane

4 *Early Military Service*

The first two years of my father's army service were spent at Maidstone where he was transferred to the 1st Battalion of the Royal West Kent regiment, having initially signed-on with the Royal Army Medical Corps. at their recruiting base in Maidstone.

During this period he befriended my uncle Henry and may have met my mother. He served in India for the next four and a half years where he had the experience of becoming lost in the desert and saw the vision described later. A short period of civilian life followed when he was transferred to the Reserve List for just two months. It was during this period that he first courted my mother.

Due to the continuing poor relationship with his father and the difficulty in securing permanent employment during the depressed pre-war days he re-joined the Army, enlisting into the Yorkshire-based Green Howards, spending the next two months at their base near Catterick, Yorks.

On 16th July 1938 the 1st Battalion Green Howards were sent to Malta where they served until October of that year before departing to Palestine. Father transferred to the 2nd Battalion Royal West Kent Regiment, then based in Malta, on 18th March 1939, just one month after I was born in Maidstone.

It was here in Malta, during the siege, that Ken spent the first four years of the war.

Aunty Blanche with mother and father in the woods –
photo by Uncle Henry.

5 *Malta*

Tuesday 11th June 1940 dawned bright and clear across Malta, as it so often did, presenting a beautiful vista for those who rose early enough to appreciate the still coolness of the island. Today was different. It was the day that war broke the silence and disturbed the usual grandeur and peace for several years to come. Air raid sirens droned their warnings. Yesterday Mussolini had declared war and Italian aircraft were soon on their way to attack Malta and Gozo.

"C" Company of the 2nd Battalion Royal West Kent Regiment were up at 0430 hrs. and about to start a new day's work building defence posts to the south west of Grand Harbour, Valetta, when the first attack took place. Soldiers quickly left their work and dropped into the narrow slit trenches dug in the soft earth of the nearby sports ground.

The noise was terrific. They could not see the clouds of dust or smoke rising from Hal-Far airfield some five miles to the south. This was the home of the few Gladiators which then formed the island's air defence. Not many minutes later, more bombers struck and destroyed buildings around the harbour itself, killing at least eight people including a mother and her two children. Such were the first two hours of war for Malta and it marked the beginning of three years of continual bombardment.

It was at this period, during the first two months of the siege, that three ageing Gladiators known locally as "Faith", "Hope" and "Charity" would fly in formation around the island, shooting down few enemy planes but raising the morale of the islanders.

One day after the first air attacks, Private Sampson learned of the sinking of one of our cruisers, HMS Calypso, by an Italian submarine fifty miles south of Crete. This made a lasting impression on him as he watched bodies being brought ashore.

The majority of soldiers in my father's regiment came through the initial onslaught unscathed although they often watched as puffs of smoke appeared around enemy aircraft from exploding shells and experienced their NAAFI tent being destroyed by fire.

Their daily routine included building machine-gun posts, digging trenches, sometimes through underlying rock, or more gruesomely, digging for survivors from the latest air raids.

The continuing bombardments caused great hardship. There was not only the physical danger from shrapnel and falling masonry, but the whole infrastructure of the island was severely disrupted. Civilians and soldiers alike frequently spent hours on end in a disused railway tunnel.

During the last few months of 1940 all the inhabitants, young and old, military and civilian, stoically carried on with their lives. Early in 1941 the British aircraft carrier HMS Illustrious docked in the Grand Harbour to give much needed air support to the well worn trio of Gladiators. The Axis powers decided, however, that Illustrious should be eliminated.

On 16th January the air raid sirens rang out once again and there followed a blitz of over one hundred Luftwaffe aircraft. The ensuing raid was described in the local press as "an Armageddon that defies description" Illustrious remained afloat in the harbour after the dust and smoke cleared, having been hit by only one bomb. The three cities that formed the ancient town of Melita, famed by St.Paul's shipwreck nearly two thousand years before, were completely destroyed.

Casualties were small due to the numerous caves and tunnels which honeycombed the old parts of the city and gave ample shelter to all who sought refuge. Day after day, almost hour after hour, the bombing continued.

One morning my father climbed over the rubble strewing and blocking the narrow streets. He saw lines of washing flapping uselessly against the remaining walls of a bombed house and noticed a family portrait picture hanging many feet in the air against an exposed wall. He remembered that yesterday children were playing in the street below.

Goats lay dead in the streets instead of being herded from door to door serving fresh milk. There was a stench in the air as newly disturbed dust rose at every slight movement of the wind or from rescuers listening for sounds of life from under the rubble.

On Saturday 18th January the Luftwaffe returned in force to reduce the newly delivered fighter aircraft now stationed at Hal-Far and Luqa. They then flew low to finish off Illustrious. Miraculously when the smoke cleared she was still afloat, her armoured deck having saved her from more serious damage.

The bombing continued unabated during the whole of 1941 and on 1st January 1942 the Nazis sent a lone bomber to deliver a New Years greeting. It was the 1,175th attack since Mussolini had sent the first waves of bombers eighteen months before.

Soldiers and civilians alike were now becoming jumpy, their nerves frayed making them "bomb happy". Some would stand in the streets or on the rooftops almost willing their lives away as more bombs rained down around them, not caring to take cover and leaving their steel hats behind as if to deny the providence of their erstwhile protection.

Food was now becoming scarce and the Mess orderlies would collect up what little left-overs there were and sweep the crumbs from the tables to supplement the next meal.

The bombing continued with 432 air raids on the island between December 1941 and January 1942 alone.

Work for the Royal West Kents was becoming exhausting as each day required more craters to be levelled from the previous bombing raids at Tikali or Luqa in addition to the urgent need to complete the building of pens to protect the aircraft.

Most of the work had to be done by hand, pick and shovel or trowel. This back-breaking work was interspersed with yet more air-raids. As the ground shook and stones and shrapnel were flung around, the soldiers would keep their heads down below the tops of the narrow slit trenches.

*Bombed apartments
in Valetta, 1941*

When the blast subsided and the dust had settled they were often faced with the dead and wounded lying helpless around them. The next job would be to clear up the mess, attending the injured where practicable. Sometimes all they could do was watch as planes burned, their crews inside screaming for help until they expired.

The trauma was often repeated and there was no counselling service in those days! So the routine continued: filling craters, building pens, taking cover, cleaning up, helping the injured and back to work. Occasionally a horse-drawn cart would stop nearby with some bread and bully-beef. Drinks were most welcome but these were always just luke-warm water.

March saw a further 275 air raids – nearly ten each day! This was more than London received in any month even during the Blitz. It was now rumoured that the Axis powers were planning to invade Malta due to the strategic position of the island in the Mediterranean. The duties of the island's militia therefore increased again in an effort to stem any sea-borne assault and this required routine patrols at night and anti-invasion exercises. Ken would often sleep in goat sheds, fields or a graveyard, plotting new positions for sangers (defence-posts) which needed to be built.

April 1942 saw Malta in a strategically hopeless position. The people were starving and the bare necessities for survival were arriving in small quantities. Most of the needed supplies now lay at the bottom of the oceans. Very few ships of the supply convoys had arrived safely. Flour, aircraft, fuel and ammunition were in desperately short supply and when these ran out the only possible course would be to surrender. The Governor sent a coded message to London asking what course should be taken and received the following reply:

*Ye shall not fear them, for the Lord your God shall fight
for you.*

(Deuteronomy 3:22)

General Dobbie, Governor General, therefore, called
upon all the people to "endure still further and to continue
to show the same courage which has won the admiration
of the world." The island people needed something
to renew their morale and on 15th April 1942 King
George VI awarded the whole population of the island
The George Cross.

The citation reads:

> *"To honour her brave people I award the
> George Cross to the island fortress of Malta
> to bear witness to a heroism and devotion to
> duty that will long be famous in history."*
>
> *George R.I*

But the bombing continued.

Raids were less frequent now, but did this herald an
invasion? May 1942 saw the first Spitfires flying around the
islands and air supremacy was slowly gained. Conditions
on land, however, scarcely improved. On Tuesday 18th June
General Dobbie issued a " Special Order of The Day".

This read:

> *"The decision of His Majesty's Government to
> fight on until our enemies are defeated will
> be heard with the greatest satisfaction by
> all ranks of the garrison of MALTA.It may be
> that hard times lie ahead of us, but however
> hard they may be I know that the courage
> and determination of all ranks will not falter*

and that with God's help we will maintain the
security of this Fortress.
I call on all Officers and Other Ranks humbly
to seek God's help and thus in reliance on Him
to do their duty unflinchingly."

N.G.Dobbie Lt. General

With more aircraft available additional duties for the militia at the aerodromes necessitated refuelling each plane manually before it could take-off again. This was only possible using four gallon jerry-cans as no tankers had survived the blitz, so ammunition, shells, bullets and bombs all had to be loaded by hand.

Ken and his comrades in arms were always hungry and the people of Malta were starving. The militia, however, had more rations than the civilian population. Daily food allowance for soldiers was just two hard – tack biscuits and a small piece of bacon for breakfast, a thin piece of corned beef for lunch and some jam for tea, which you were supposed to eat with a piece of biscuit saved from breakfast. Tea was rationed to three cups a day.

Sometimes a meal cart would pull up with soup, so thin that the bottom of the cauldron would be visible. Corned beef was sometimes served in different guises but was so monotonous, however cooked, that it was regarded boring despite the gnawing hunger of the troops.

Fruit was very scarce and a black market developed. Local farmers could charge a whole week's wages for an egg sandwich. When not too tired, soldiers were to be found scrumping for melons or stealing a chicken or even a goat for the pot.

Some of the injuries sustained from bomb blasts were horrific and limbs, torsos and even heads would be severed from the bodies to which they once belonged. Each had to be loaded onto a cart destined for the mortuary.

By the end of 1942 Malta had become the most bombed place on earth.

6 *North Africa*

1943 saw a turning of the tides of war and the island fortress was gradually turning into a staging post for the assaults of our forces into North Africa and the Middle East. With frayed nerves my father left Malta on 10th June 1943 for a posting in Alexandria still with the Royal West Kent Regiment. He was to be to be redeployed for further action.

On 19th June, his Battalion was to be found at a transit camp at Sidi Bishr from whence they went to Syria for training and then on to Jezreel in Palestine and Kibrit in Egypt for further Combined Operations training until 19th September 1943. Father clearly failed to impress his senior officers at this stage and was left behind in Haifa when most of the Battalion sailed in a destroyer to Samos and Leros. He was back in England and posted to the 13th Infantry Training Corps. Then at Invicta Lines in Maidstone on 6th November 1943.

The next three months could have seen Ken visit home at Christmas time or during a period of leave when I would have been four and a half years old but I have no recollection of any visit or contact and my mother always maintained that she never saw him during the whole of the war. This may have been due to the strict security measures in force at the time as it was only to be a matter of months before the allies invaded Normandy. No one had ever heard of D-Day then.

In February 1944 my father was transferred to 2nd. Battalion
East Surrey Regiment, stationed "somewhere in England".

British troops marching to the front line in Normandy.

7 *Normandy*

The D-Day Invasion of Normandy began on the evening of 5th June 1944 when the 2nd Battalion Oxfordshire and Buckinghamshire Light Infantry (Ox & Bucks) stormed the Orne Canal bridge at Benouville after the successful landing of their Airborne Division who put down their gliders alongside the canal.

"Pegasus Bridge", as it became known, was taken out of German hands at one minute past midnight on 6th June. This success cost the Regiment two lives with only four men injured. A quite remarkable start to what was later to become some of the bloodiest fighting of the war during the next ten weeks.

Madame Gondray and her young daughter were up early that morning to serve breakfast to our troops and that young lady proudly serves English and Canadian visitors at the same café to this day. Now grey-haired, she was autographing maps and memoirs for tourists during our visit in August 2006.

The 2nd Battalion then fought their way eastwards across the River Dives towards the Seine as they proceeded en-route to Paris, encountering increasing resistance from the Germans.

The 1st Battalion Oxfordshire & Buckinghamshire Light Infantry (Ox & Bucks) landed in Normandy at Courseulles-sur-Mer on 24th and 25th June 1944. My father disembarked at the remaining Mulberry Harbour at Arromanches which was in use until 19th November. He was then with the 33rd Reinforcement Holding Regiment awaiting his last posting and arrived on 16th July. He was moved to the battle zone in half-tracked troop carriers or sometimes marching with full kit and rifle through marked minefields.

He was transferred to 1st Battalion Ox.& Bucks on 25th July 1944 and was attached to A Company where he joined that unit somewhere between Monceux and Bougy where they were regrouping following the Battle for Cahier (now known as Cayer).

Instructions were received on 14th July to attack Cahier whilst the Battalion was encamped at Le Hout de Bosq. It was thought that the Germans possibly had a Battalion H.Q. in the vicinity.

This battle started at 0300 hrs. and was fought in darkness and in difficult terrain with no artillery or air support. It was truly an infantryman's battle and they reached the high ground overlooking a mill in a deep and narrow valley on the small River Odon.

Soon mortar fire was brought to bear by the enemy and an order to clear the mill resulted in hand-to-hand fighting. Captain Cooper entered the dark interior of the mill and bayoneted several Germans before being killed, himself. In this battle the 1st Battalion lost 9 officers and 166 other ranks. The Germans lost 254 with 116 wounded. The British took 138 prisoners.

The Germans, meanwhile, were preparing to retaliate, not many miles away to the east of Caen where the 1st and 21st Panzer Divisions were stationed.

Between 17th and 20th July the Allies launched an unprecedented attack with a thousand-bomber raid to the east of Caen to soften the Nazi presence there, followed by a naval bombardment of the same scale. Villers-Bocage and Aunay-sur-Odon were pulverised by the RAF. At this time there were many civilian casualties.

Meanwhile three divisions of our XII Corps moved east to hold the crossings over the Orne bridges. Also "Operation Goodwood" was organised to advance along the Caen to Falaise road in an attempt to penetrate the considerable Caen fortifications.

The noise from the Battle for Caen was so loud that it was heard from the English coast. Air support continued with our rocket-firing Typhoons knocking out lines of German armour wherever they could be targeted, all this in close proximity to our own advancing infantry units. Chaos surrounded our troops, with vehicles ablaze and the dead and injured spread around the roads, fields and woods; indeed wherever one looked.

Rommel now ordered General Rundstedt "to push the invaders back into the sea". Montgomery ordered "Operation Bluecoat" and from 30th July through to 6th August fierce battles were fought at Argentan, Auney-sur-Odon and on the Caen to Vire road.

The Americans meanwhile were driving from the south to form a pincer movement against the Nazi advance.

The German 7th Army with their 5th Panzer Army now found themselves in a great salient, where our troops had advanced into what had been enemy territory. To the north was our 21st Army Group led by General Montgomery! As the British and Canadians moved in, the salient was closed to become a pocket known as "The Falaise Gap". The enemy now had little choice but to move towards the east, but not without a fight. They were pounded from the air and their units were surrounded and surrendering.

With all cohesion now gone the great German retreat was underway. They suffered appalling casualties in men, machines and horses. German losses totalled more than 140,000 men in the battles for Normandy.

Where was my Dad in all of this?

"Rocket-firing Typhoons at the Falaise Gap, Normandy, 1944" by Frank Wootton. Crown Copyright.

8 *The Falaise Gap*

Father joined the 1st Battalion Ox and Bucks Light Infantry and found them recovering from the devastation they had suffered during the battle for Cahier. They stayed at Bougy, a mile and a half North of Evrecy for two days watching from a distance the ongoing slaughter of the Germans a few miles to the South. Whilst there they were in close contact with the enemy, several German deserters walked into the British lines during the next few days.

Battle Orders were drawn for 30th July when six companies were grouped at Bougy. The enemy paid them quite a bit of attention by way of artillery and mortar fire and a small raid forward was planned with artillery and mortar support. This was called off due to sudden heavy machine gunning and mortar fire from close range.

A few days of respite were spent overlooking Evrecy after the enemy withdrew although there was considerable activity by the RAF whose Typhoons were firing rockets and dropping bombs close by. Four soldiers of the regiment were killed and nine injured in a "friendly fire" incident. The smell of battle was all around and with the rotting corpses of dead horses as well as the remnants of the grey battledress of dead Germans who had not managed to retreat. The scene was one of indescribable horror to be etched indelibly in the mind of my father and his comrades in arms.

From 9th August the 1st Battalion marched to Bougy ready to move off and on the 10th they marched four miles south to St. Honorine du Fay.

A line of a dozen lorries arrived soon after first light at their encampment at St. Honorine. The troops were assembling for departure and my father noticed the white stars painted on the doors of each truck besmirched with sandy dust from the roads as he followed his platoon mates and swung himself up from the single knotted rope hanging from the rear canvas cover rail into the darkened interior. They made themselves as comfortable as packs and rifles would allow and their nostrils soon became choked with the pungency of new paint and oily canvas that perfumed the interior, mixed with the ever present exhaust fumes from the truck. All allied vehicles were marked with the white star to allow easy identification by our attacking aircraft.

Nervousness gripped them and it seemed a long time before the engine burst into life, their destination unknown. The narrow roads through Bretteville and Trois Monts mocked them as the choking dust mixed with exhaust fumes swirled into the open backs of the trucks. A few parched throats began to croak, "It's a long way to Tipperary" when the tension could be felt to subside a little.

By the time the driver changed to a lower gear and they started to descend into a deep valley, it had seemed like a long journey, and they were glad it had not been a foot slog as so often had been the case since their arrival in France.

The last few hundred yards were completed in low gear as the driver had difficulty in negotiating the carpet of branches that had been shattered from their overhang to lay in the roadway. The denuded branches pointed heavenward like fingers, the result of recent shellfire.

From the point where they de-bussed they could see a new Bailey Bridge spanning the gap where until recently three of the five stone arches of Le Pont du Brie had crossed The Orne and over which they would soon march to get closer to the enemy.

Le Pont du Brie from the west bank of the Orne –
Bailey Bridge in-situ

The Foret du Cinglais afforded much leafy cover and the regiment marched to the north-west corner of the wood in hot and dusty conditions, the temperature rising to 90 deg.F even in the shade. The troops were carrying heavy packs and all of their armaments firstly in unbearable heat and later during hours of darkness.

Flies became a problem along with the awful smell of rotting carcases of cattle and human corpses. Some of the men were sick with diarrhoea and the marching at night was difficult as they continued along narrow tracks with dense undergrowth where their faces were torn by briars and their feet sore and blistered from the activity of the past days.

A camaraderie developed between the men which none of them had hitherto experienced. They would now rather stay with their chosen comrades regardless of safety or comfort than take any safer option that might present itself. The transport vehicles carrying food and ammunition became lost in the darkness of the forest as they were unable to use headlamps due to now being in enemy occupied territory. The Germans were still in Espin and Fresnay-les-Vieux, less than two miles away.

Bois Halbout had been captured on 12th August and A and C Companies were ordered to relieve the 1st Battalion East Lancs. Regiment and take up a new start line in a quarry half a mile to the South. As they were transported through Bois Halbout the remains of a burned out vehicle, with the charred body of the driver in the cab, still stood at the roadside, a grim reminder of what they could soon possibly be facing. The smell of burning oil and steel hung heavily in the air. Some of the men in C Company happily found and tapped a barrel of cider that evening and shared it with their Platoon mates. Some slept well that night!

Before dawn on Sunday 13th August, my father, with A Company, established themselves in the quarry to await reinforcements. The quarry, midway between Bois Halbout and La Bijude is still there today, although partly filled in.

In the event C Company, the reinforcements, were delayed having lost one vehicle due to shellfire.

9 *La Bijude*

On Sunday morning 13th August in the hours before first light, Colonel James Hare was ordered to take the crossroads at La Bijude, half a mile to the south of the quarry where they had rested overnight. This action was to be done to gain as much advantage as possible before sunrise.

Each Company had its own objective but their routes were not generally known and they were to advance at half hourly intervals. The strength of opposition was uncertain. As the troops moved forward in classic infantry formation they heard little and found themselves in a thick mist as the sun rose. Some doubted the presence of an enemy until they heard the sound of picks and spades in the cornfield to the left of the road.

A soldier walking quickly in the wrong direction whispered to those advancing, "Germans". It was clear that the enemy didn't know they were there and were very quickly dealt with. Most became prisoners and were sent back to the base at the quarry. Quite suddenly the morning sun penetrated the mist and they were exposed to view. To their horror they discovered they had passed the furthest German outposts in the mist and immediately a close small arms battle with cross-fire was fought. A number of the combatants on both sides fell.

Two Tiger Tanks of the 21st Panzer Division were standing on the road beside the farm buildings to the south. One opened fire with a machine gun straight down the road. Men dived into the cover of shallow ditches at the roadsides.

Many were wounded and six were killed. This initial battle continued unabated for four hours. Sergeant Kirk killed 3 Germans and took 6 prisoners from a position 30 yards to the south of the cross-roads where the enemy occupied some stables. He was awarded the Military Medal for this action.

Meanwhile Major Callaghan killed a German patrol and took several prisoners before shooting a leading officer at 5 yards range. Many more men were wounded. At 10:00 hrs. the order was given to withdraw to the start line. Lieutenant Stanley Middlebrook refused to go back, however, until he had accounted for each of his men. My father had meanwhile been detailed to a Carrier, took a Bren gun and secured it to the mounts. Nervously he repeated under his breath the drill he was so familiar with.

> *"Gun stops firing one, change magazine, gun*
> *stops firing two, change barrel..."*

In the minutes remaining before receiving orders to move, his mind may have wandered back to childhood and he wondered if, on this Sunday morning, his mother and father would remember him in their prayers at the church where he had once sung in the choir. He wondered too whether Lucy, my mother, would want him when he returned home. What too had become of his baby boy? His brother? His sister?

That afternoon A and D Companies were ordered to attack and it was now that my father moved forward in the Bren-gun carrier towards the crossroads. The tracked vehicle was heavily loaded with cases of ammunition, containing the curved magazines for the Bren guns now on board. The crew were apprehensive and very alert. There was a strong smell of cordite as they edged forward through the battle smoke.

Fierce fighting was going on ahead and a PIAT anti tank mortar was fired to destroy one of the two tanks still in the road near the farmyard. It was blazing furiously as my father's Bren carrier moved unsteadily from the road to follow the edge of the cornfield towards their objective.

They were soon fired on by a Schmeiser near the farm and once or twice had to make an evasive manoeuvre to avoid being hit by this much feared German machine-gun. The carrier rattled its way relentlessly through the cornfield heading towards the cross-roads and the burning farm a few hundred yards in front of them.

A wounded officer being carried on a stretcher to a waiting jeep was heard to shout, "Send Shelldrake, I implore you, send Shelldrake" (wireless guided artillery). He was still fighting a war despite his injuries.

My father's carrier drove on until suddenly there was a blinding flash and then darkness. The carrier had run over an anti-tank mine! Some time later my father became conscious, the sound of Shelldrake whining overhead. He could not see the remains of his carrier which had become the funeral pyre of all but one his erstwhile comrades, as he lay, semi-conscious, on a low bank close to the road where he had been thrown by the explosion.

Later the two survivors were picked up by a passing Jeep and taken to the Regimental Aid Post before being transported to a casualty clearing station in the orchard next to the farm at La Bijude.

The Battle for Normandy was considered to be over on 15th August 1944. My Dad's war was now over too. He was sent back to England, on 16th August, to a hospital at Chertsey, where he arrived a few days later, a broken man.

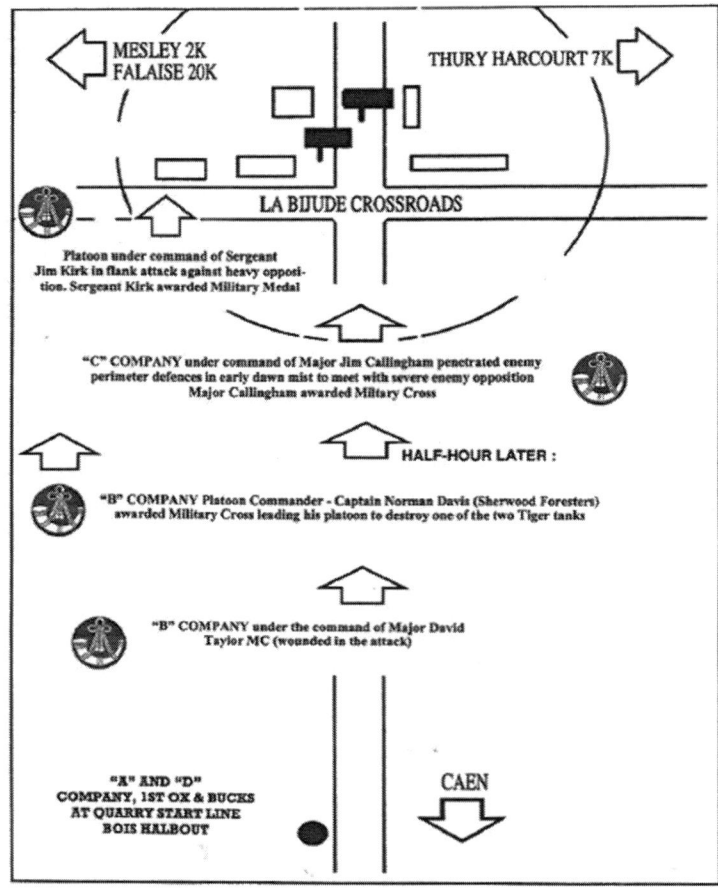

LA BIJUDE CROSS-ROADS - 13TH AUGUST 1944

The 1st Battalion, East Lancashire Regiment captured German positions around the quarry at Bois Halbout and established a base start line from which the 1st Ox & Bucks mounted their attack on the crossroads at La Bijude. The objective stood on commanding ground on the road from Bretteville sur Laize to Pont D'ouilly where it was crossed by another from Falaise to Thury Harcourt. Preliminary intelligence suggested light opposition but in the event it was severe, supported by two Tiger tanks, one of which was destroyed in the initial assault by "B" and "C" Company. Such was the intensity of the fighting that both companies were withdrawn to allow an artillery barrage to precede and support "A" and "D" Company moving forward with armoured assistance to eventually take the objective

With no post-trauma counselling, his nerves in shreds and with some physical injuries, a psychosis of retreat overtook his mind. Father was later transferred to a mental hospital in Carstairs and was discharged from the Army as unfit for further military service five months later on 30th January 1945. Nowadays servicemen are treated for Post Traumatic Stress Disorder. In the 1st World War they were often shot for desertion. In the 2nd World War they were discharged as medically unfit for service!

The battle described is but one of similar incidents that took place during the whole of this campaign before the advancing Canadians took Falaise on 15th August 1944.

On visiting the farmhouse at La Bijude during the summer of 2006, Iris and I knocked at the front door which was shortly opened a little and we were faced by a small lady who eyed us inquisitively. Iris's Germanic ancestry may have shown through her smiling face with high cheek-bones, as I explained that we were researching the battle that was fought here in August 1944. At first I thought that we were going to have the door closed on us but after a poignant silence, the French lady said" Vous êtes Anglais", "oui, oui", I replied quickly.

"Entrez dans monsieur et madame!"

From that moment we were welcomed in and shown many artefacts from that skirmish and escorted around the old farmstead with enthusiasm to view the scars of the battle and shown where Nazi soldiers had been hiding in pig-styes in wait for the British.

My mother received an Army travel pass for two to Scotland and early in February she travelled by rail with my paternal grandmother to find her husband, only to be informed that Kenneth Sampson had discharged himself a few days earlier.

My father then became one of the many homeless to roam the towns, streets and lanes of this country following his military service.. He had neither the will or ability to make a claim on the government of the day and so lived on his wits for the next twenty-eight years.

Thus began the years of silence for us. The war was still on and travel and money scarce. My mother also had a five year old son to bring up on her own. My father's whereabouts remained uncertain until 1972.

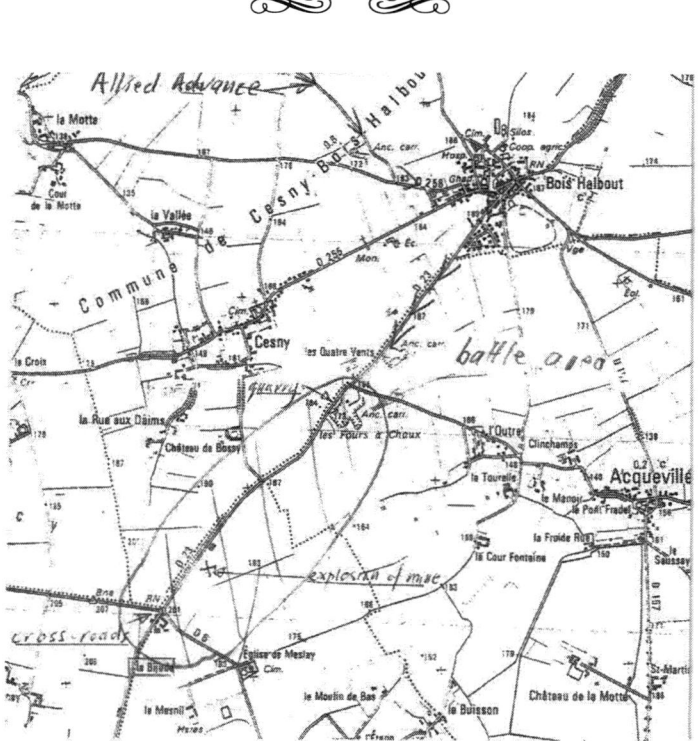

Footnote: The battle described above should not be confused with that which took place nearer the coast at Le Bijude on 28th June 1944.

10 *The Commission*

IIIIIIIIIIIIIIIIIIIIIIIIIIIIIIIIIIIIIIIIIIIIIIIIIIIIIIIIIIIIIIIIIIIIIIIIIIIIIIIIIIIIIIIIIIIIIIIIIIIIIIIIII

My early working life was spent in Maidstone, where early in 1959 I met Iris, who, three years later, was to become my wife. Then only seventeen years of age, she turned out to be the perfect choice for someone destined to experience a most unusual life as a wife and mother. Without her sympathetic understanding, her love and loyal devotion to the cause, later to be laid upon us, this story would not be told.

Our early married life was spent in our new home in Burham, situated beneath the North Downs between Maidstone and Rochester, high above the Medway valley. It was here, when our first two children, Mark and Beverley were infants, that John and would spend evenings together and I suppose my social conscience was awakened.

During 1968 we started to attend a Baptist Chapel in Chatham and the next four years saw a slow change in the patterns of our lives as we attempted to align our ideals with those we heard regularly preached faithfully from the Bible. This was a struggle because of the conflict with our ambitions to succeed in business and to enjoy all that this world affords. Notwithstanding we became a respectable 2+2 family in our home surroundings and enjoyed a comfortable standard of living with annual holidays abroad. I became a parish councillor, school governor and a scout leader within the village.

Early in 1972 we arranged to sit with the children of my friend John and his wife Lois to enable them to attend a church meeting to give their testimonies when applying for baptism. During that evening in their home Iris and I prayed for our friends and read the Bible together. Our thoughts were for John and Lois's good and for their acceptance into the church. A few minutes before they returned I opened the scriptures and read from the Acts of the Apostles 2:17:

> 'Now when they heard this they were pricked in their
> hearts and said unto Peter and to the rest of the apostles,
> "men and brethren, what shall we do?" Then Peter said
> unto them repent and be baptised every one of you in
> the name of Jesus Christ for the remission of sins and ye
> shall receive the gift of the Holy Ghost. For this promise
> is to you and to your children and to all THAT ARE
> AFAR OFF even as many as The Lord our God shall call'

These words fell with great meaning into our hearts but before closing the Bible, the verses to be found at the end of Ecclesiastes 12 also leapt out of the page:

> "Let us hear the conclusion of the whole matter, fear God
> and keep his commandments for this is the whole duty
> of man"

An angel stood in the corner of the room announcing this as the word from God for us to take hold of for eternity. We both knew that our lives could not be the same again and that we would have to follow God's commands in whatever He called us to do. Iris and I were both baptised by immersion at Enon Chapel, Chatham by the Pastor, Leslie Jarvis, in May that year in obedience to the Divine command. It was but a few weeks later that we were challenged by God in our consciences.

"Here you are professing to know your Heavenly Father, but you do not even know the whereabouts of your earthly father" said a still small voice. This message came to me repeatedly but I kept it to myself for weeks. One evening on returning home from work however, Iris asked me why I had been so quiet lately.

She then told me that she knew, and that she shared a concern for my father. The Holy Spirit had clearly been working in two souls simultaneously without any human prompting. We then knew what God's commission was for us and from that day forward we set our hearts and minds on locating my earthly father.

And so the story unfolds.

11 *Found*

||||||||||||||||||||||||||||||||||||||||||||||||||||||||||||||||||||||||||||||||||||||||||||||||||||||||||||||||||||||||||||||||||

At 7.35 a.m. on 1st July 1972 I was sitting in our pastor's car with him opposite the side door to Pentonville Jail in Wheelwright Street, London. I had been advised to arrive early as the release of prisoners, due at 8 o'clock, could be pre-empted if the day staff arrived early for duty.

The morning was grey and cold and somehow reflected the apprehensive mood that I felt.

Mother had been passed a letter from my father, addressed to Uncle Henry, at our old home, in which he wrote that he would like to come to Kent to go hop-picking upon his release. I tried to locate my uncle but he was on holiday in Italy at that time. The letter was clearly inspired by the prison welfare department.

This was the culmination of three weeks of ardent prayer, during which we determined not to post the letters Iris had typed to various missing persons bureaux, believing that God would hear and respond to our petitions.

The narrow door opened and out stepped four figures with
their heads bowed. Pastor Leslie and I crossed the road to meet
them face to face. One must be my father. The two younger of
the party strode forward to leave the older men behind them.
Which one was my Dad? The fellow on the inside with the
thin face resembled what I could remember of him from early
photographs in Mother's albums. He wore a dark brown great-
coat held together with a ragged necktie and he smelled.

"Are you Kenneth Sampson?" I asked; "I am Peter, your
son." "No" he blurted out, and without hesitation ran to the
corner of the main road and crossed it, endeavouring to give
us the slip as he disappeared into the entrance of Caledonian
Road underground station. Leslie and I were only able to
catch up with him due to his being delayed while purchasing
a ticket to Baker Street.

Before the ticket collector was able to inspect it I offered
a five pound note if he would come with us. At this his eyes
lit up but he repeatedly said "Baker Street, Baker Street". I
promised to take him to Baker Street knowing that there is
a street with the same name in our village. Reluctantly he
walked with us to the waiting car.

That moment the realisation of the weighty responsibility
I was taking on hit me as the vile odour of stale alcohol,
tobacco and urine combined to perfume the inside of
Leslie's car with such strength that necessitated opening all
the windows.

The prison authorities confiscate every item of the inmates
clothing and seal them all in a black plastic bag until the
day of release, hence the awful smell! How could I take
this wreck of humanity home to meet my wife and young
children? Should I quit now and leave him to the life he was
so used to?

I turned to where he sat uncomfortably in the back seat
and asked, "Pop, what do you most want now?", thinking it

may be food or a drink. "Most of all I want my self respect back" he muttered, through black teeth. I instantly knew that there could be no turning back now.

Leslie drove through London as Pop mumbled the various place names as we passed. We travelled along the Old Kent Road and stopped for some refreshment at a "greasy spoon" adjacent to New Cross Station, believing correctly that Pop, as I now began to call him, would be hungry. I ordered three teas, two breakfasts and some toast for Leslie. We sat on plastic chairs at a corner table with bowls containing congealed brown globules of sugar and sticky bottles of vinegar and brown and red sauces. There was litter on the floor from days past. Suddenly I found myself almost retching with nausea from the awful stench of my father's impregnated coat. Pop devoured both breakfasts and Leslie left his toast as we rose to wait outside. I think Pop ate the toast too.

The next leg of the journey into Kent finished at my friend John's home in Gillingham where I had left my car earlier that morning. John and his family received us gracefully.

Philip, John's younger son, asked his mother why they couldn't find an old tramp to help, as Pop willingly peeled some potatoes that were being prepared for their dinner!

John came home with me to see if we could clean the old tramp up a bit and I was pleased to find our house empty when we arrived. Iris was still out shopping with our children Mark and Beverley and they never did see him in his original dishevelled condition.

John put his ambulance training to good effect as we stood Pop on newspapers on the kitchen floor and undressed him. I rolled up the clothes dousing them with petrol and burned the stinking bundle on a bonfire at the bottom of the garden while John retired with him to the bathroom to clean him up in a hot bath while I found some clothing.

When the family arrived home Pop was respectably dressed, sitting on the settee in our lounge and sipping a whisky, the only drink that I had to offer for his homecoming celebration.

It was difficult to elicit any sensible conversation with this erstwhile vagrant as he always mumbled and constantly repeated his words. I did, however, get a response from him as to why he had taken to his heels when I met him earlier in the day.

"Thought that you were disreputable men after my money," he said. (The money in question was the one day of Social Security pay given to all prisoners upon their release.)

On their return from the shopping trip Iris, Mark and Beverley were introduced to Pop and there were kisses and tears all around.

As my father was very restless and not being used to settling anywhere for more than a few hours I decided to take the now enlarged family to the Sittingbourne and Kemsley Light Railway for the afternoon, hoping to rekindle a new interest in my father's life.

Old habits, especially those formed over half a lifetime, die hard and Pop would instinctively know, and let us know too, whenever the pubs were open. The learning curve in those first few days was difficult and would inevitably be steep if we were to cope with one who had had no aims in life for twenty eight years and who was prone to walk away whenever he faced something unusual or disagreeable.

Pop was kitted out with jacket, trousers, pullovers and underwear as he eagerly opened the small case given to him on the first Sunday after he was found. The clothes all fitted his thin frame as the previous owner had had a slight figure. Our Pastor, Leslie, gave these to Pop as they had been left to him by his father-in law, recently deceased. We saw this as a wonderful provision at the appropriate time.

One startling feature, having found a father, previously unknown to me, was how alike we were in mannerisms. I soon observed that I held my hands in the same mode as Pop did when describing something, and the angle of my head very often mimicked his under similar circumstances. This proved to me, genetic heredity, rather than the assimilation of characteristics whilst living close to one's parents.

Pop and Beverley – Kent Showground, July 1972

12 *Burham*

Mother's face was all smiles as she hurried from the bus to our home. She was expectant as she greeted father, having last seen him some twenty five years before. We left them in our lounge for their reunion but when Mother emerged she had tears in her eyes. "This is not the man I married," was her sad response. I took her home in silence.

Our home at Burham had a small garden and the following Saturday, 8th July 1972 we spent the afternoon weeding and tidying the borders. Pop helped with the chores for some time before asking if he could go for a walk around the village. Wearing his new jacket and tie he set off up the road alone. We expected him back to tea but he did not return.

Before dusk I had already traversed all the routes he may have taken around our village and into the neighbouring villages of Wouldham and Eccles, but to no avail. After dark I phoned John to share our concerns for the old chap. John thought that he would miss his comfortable bed. We left the house unlocked, lights on in strategic locations, in the hope that he would be there in the morning. Then we prayed.

A trail of hay on the stairs gave away his previous night's activities and he said he had slept in a good hay barn but came home when it got cold! Another answer to our prayers.

There were five pubs in Burham village and Pop soon became known at each one. At first I thought that Pop was suffering from alcoholism but it soon became clear that his habitual requirement to visit a public house was to seek the only warmth and comfort that he had known for the past twenty-eight years. After all these were the only opportunities he had been able to make to receive any nourishment for his thin body. Escaping from our sight each morning at 10.30 if our attention was diverted, he would find his way into either the Windmill or the Royal Albert in the main street.

I was chairman of the Parish Council at the time and knew each of the Landlords. They readily agreed to phone us if Pop arrived so that I could retrieve him before any nuisance was caused or before he wandered further afield, and also so that I could pay for the beer he may have consumed in the interim! Pop had no money of his own during those first weeks with us.

One morning a fortnight later he was gone again. Where to, or why, remained a mystery. The only clues were some of the words constantly muttered under his breath, "Finchley Road", "Middle Wallop", "Wolverhampton" and "Swiss Cottage".

At this time our young son Mark needed to visit Guy's Hospital for a check on his recurring skin condition and a visit was due three days later. On that morning Mark asked his Mum to make up Grandad's bed as he knew that we would find him. Why? Because we had prayed that he would come back and Mark thought that we would find him in London! I was afraid that my young child's faith would be shattered if we were unsuccessful and so prayed all the way and asked for the guidance of an all-knowing God to enable us to find Pop again.

The visit to the hospital was over by midday. What should we do now? I decided that a ride on the underground would please the children and so we set off for Swiss Cottage. A few yards from the station there was then a small area of green with a swing, a roundabout and a couple of benches. Iris stayed there with Mark and Beverley and I asked her to pray whilst I searched the local public bars, promising to return within an hour. It was pleasantly warm as I looked across the road towards the outside tables at the Swiss Cottage pub but there were only a few early lunchtime drinkers there.

So I turned the corner into Finchley Road to face a sea of people hurriedly engaged in their lunchtime pursuits. I thought that I could see a tramp-like figure some hundred yards away. Were my eyes leading me to imagine I could see what I was hoping for?

No. It really was Pop, slouching along towards me! He held his arms wide on recognising me and in greeting said, "It's like the prodigal son in reverse." Iris and the children could hardly believe their eyes and instantly wept with joy.

The pockets of the old railwayman's jacket he wore were stuffed with a quart cider bottle and newspapers, a necktie around his middle. Odd shoes and wet trousers betrayed his return to the vagrancy that we were endeavouring to release him from. Passengers on the Bakerloo Line could scarcely believe the sight as we sat, an old tramp between a weeping man and woman, each with a small child at their side on the side seat of the swaying tube train.

Early one Sunday morning the phone rang. It was our local policeman who asked if we had an old gentleman staying with us. "My father", I replied in the affirmative. There was a short pause before the PC asked if we were aware that he had a criminal record. I knew little about my father's life but told him that I had retrieved him from Pentonville a few weeks earlier. I visited the Police House every village had one in those days) and was shown a Telex from the Metropolitan Police indicating sixteen entries from the Criminal Records Office. These were mainly for begging and vagrancy, i.e. having no visible means of support. There was one for stealing a bicycle for which he was committed to Bedford Jail for a three month term and one for possessing an offensive weapon.

It turned out that he was caught for the bicycle offence because someone had told him to leave Cambridge before he became a nuisance. He saw a bicycle leaning against the wall of a butcher's shop and promptly rode away into the country. The following day conscience got the better of him and he rode it back again only to be arrested and jailed for his simplicity! The offensive weapon was a folding penknife in his pocket!

Pop later told us that he once threw a brick into a shop window in Edmonton to get into prison for Christmas. Such was life on the road.

Having taken stock of our new commitment to look after an ageing vagrant we became concerned about the state of his health and made an appointment for him to be examined by our own GP. "If you are as healthy as your father when you get to his age you will be very lucky", pronounced the doctor. We were relieved for the sake of our children.

Then there were his black and rotting teeth. I well remember the sight of my Dad walking down Star Hill Rochester after a visit to Mr. Henriques, the dentist, blood running from the corners of his mouth, smiling and muttering, "laughing gas, laughing gas". The dentures followed later!

Lifting the top of Mark's desk at Primary School, I opened his English book. The last essay was his perspective of family life. It read of happy times, outings to the sea, walks in the country, and games with friends, but my vision became blurred with tears as I came to the last sentence. "Then my grandad came".

When we first found Pop I cancelled our proposed holiday to St. Michel-en-Greve on the Normandy coast and instead made arrangements to stay in a Christian Guest House in Shropshire for a week. Cloverley Hall was a grand house set in acres of parkland and Pop had a great time, playing table tennis, swimming and watching me fall into the lake when attempting to climb into a canoe too small for my hips! Did he laugh!

Pop was very good at table tennis and his long arms seemed to enable his bat to be just at the right place to return each ball swiftly. I remember well, however, that he was not too impressed by the length of our evening devotional prayer times and more than once we heard a dull thud as the heavy door from the dining room swung closed as Pop was trying to make an escape between the trees in the parkland and out onto the nearby road.

A quick and quiet pursuit each time followed to resolve the status quo! One afternoon we traversed the nearby countryside by car and on entering a town, Pop announced, "this is Bridgnorth; Crown on the right and Falcon on the left."

"Have you been here before then, Pop?" I asked.

"I've been in every town and village in England," he retorted.

I later found this to be almost literally true. We naively

believed that my Dad would now settle down. We were soon to learn that his tramping habits would die hard.

Iris and Pop at Cloverley Hall

Colonel Slight,
Salvation Army,
110 Middlesex Street,
London E1.

51, Whitehouse Crescent,
Burham,
Rochester,
Kent.
Tel: Medway 62929
(STD 0634)

31st. July 1972.

Dear Colonel Slight,

Further to our recent telephone conversation concerning my father, I am listing below some details which I hope you will find relevant with view to tracing him:-

NAME.	Kenneth Ewart SAMPSON.
Date of birth.	14th. November 1910.
Height.	5'-7".
Weight.	10st. 6 lb.
Hair.	receding, greying ginger.
Eyes.	Blue/grey.
Last seen.	21st. July when he left here.
Dressed as follows:-	
	Black shoes.
	Light grey trousers.
	Dark grey jacket.
	Green jersey.
	Shirt and tie.

Mr. Sampson was discharged from the Armed Forces with a mental breakdown in 1946. After some medical treatment he was unable to settle to home life and disappeared, early in 1947. During the past twenty-five years his whereabouts have been unknown to my mother and I except for the two occasions when he has contacted us whilst serving short term prison sentences, usually for begging, the last time being in 1959.

Early this year my wife and I became concerned about his welfare, and after much prayerful deliberation we discovered, on 29th. June last, that he was serving 14 days imprisonment at Pentonville (prison no. 110793). He was released on 1st. July when I met him and he returned here to live with us.

He was very concerned that we would help him to restore his self respect, and with this in view he was undergoing dental treatment and has had his teeth removed. As yet he has no dentures.

We are now very anxious to trace my father again as we believe that we can help him and any assistance that you can give to this end will be much appreciated. Enclosed is a recent photograph of my father and daughter.

I am enclosing a small donation to help defray any expenses in this connection.

Yours sincerely,

P.J.E. Sampson.

13 *London Again*

At the end of July 1972 the lounge window was open one morning and there was no sign of Pop. What time he had left home was a mystery, for we had not heard a sound. John and I searched our locality the next day to no avail. More prayers were offered.

One Saturday our friend Steve joined John and I and all three of us went to London where we had found Pop before. We walked along Finchley Road from Swiss Cottage to the underground station and covered the ground bounded by Belsize Park, Chalk Farm and St. Johns Wood stations. We looked in all the likely bars, down cellar steps and on door plates for an elusive Norma Swinburn, a name that we often heard muttered in a low breath! Footsore and tired we were on the brink of calling it a day when we peered into a crowded bar. It was quiet save for the gabble of a myriad of revellers when suddenly "Amazing Grace" blared out from the stage. Turning towards me John said, "God moves in a mysterious way", and so we resumed our search until the end of the day, sadly to no avail. However it was with renewed spirits and faith in our mission that we returned home.

The following day a prayer meeting was held at Chapel for Pop's safe return and on 31st July I wrote another letter, this time to the Salvation Army, a copy of which is included within this book. We really had no idea where my Father may have gone but felt inclined to look once more in the places to where he seemed to gravitate and so at the next opportunity I went again with Iris and my mother to visit the Finchley Road area.

We were encouraged when I spoke to a flower seller who stood outside Swiss Cottage tube station. Yes, he had seen the old tramp who used to be a regular in the area. "Someone has cleaned him up a bit" he said, "but he was around yesterday". I gave him a bank note together with my phone number and requested him to ring us if he spotted the old tramp again.

With renewed hope we walked up and down Finchley Road trying to imagine what Pop may have been doing during this lunch hour. We booked a table in a Restaurant where we could sit in the window, keeping an eye out for the one we were looking for, and quietly pray. Before the waiter brought our food I was able to invite that vagrant to dine with us! Good manners persisted and nobody moved away from the aroma of three weeks of homeless living and vagrancy emanating from the table by the window.

14 *Holiday Times*

During the summers of 1973 and 1974 we booked a self-catering holiday at Pen-y-Craig, the home of Mr and Mrs Richards, near Amroth in Wales, very near the end of the Pembroke Coast Path. As well as their own cottage, with its solid fuel Aga, there was a pair of converted covered railway wagons which we thought would be ideal both for our children and for Pop. The accommodation was ample and the first year we invited my mother to come with us. It was during this time that there was a stricken petrol tanker the Donna Marika, which had run aground off Milford Haven.

We followed the coast path to a point where we could see at close quarters the listing vessel, still leaking its cargo into the sea. The air was pungent with the smell of petrol vapour and there were numerous signs posted, as well as a patrol of coastguards, to ensure that there were no naked lights or cigarettes being lit in the vicinity. Pop, however, did not seem to understand the import of the danger and we had great difficulty in making him see that he had to go without a cigarette for a while, to the point that we had to cut short our coastal walk.

Early one evening, as we were returning from a long walk on the Prescelly Hills, Pop called our attention to a lamb with its head stuck firmly in the wire of a stock fence. As we approached it became frantic and was in danger of injury.

Pop carefully restrained its body whilst Mark and I bent the wire to release its head. It soon ran away bleating for is mother. Pop smiled all the way back to the car!

It was during this time away that we realised the gulf that then existed between my mother and father. Pop wanted to be a friendly husband to mother while she seemed to want to dominate aspects of his life. My dear Iris became a very good counsellor to Pop and was able to keep the peace between them for the most part. A great contrast to events described later.

We visited many rural parts of Pembrokeshire and there were many times when Pop let us know that he had been there before. A photo. shoot was necessary when we stumbled upon three little girls in Welsh costume who could not speak English near a farm named Sampson! Pop came close to giving us the slip more than once but I managed to prevent another get-away, especially at Cenarth where he nearly hid in a mill!

On holiday in Pembrokeshire

On a day trip to London where Pop renews an old acquaintance

The following year we repeated our booking at Pen-y-Craig but this time went with two families from our chapel, Enon, Chatham. Steve and Miriam Casse and Tony and Valerie Morris, each with their children. Steve and Tony had become involved in looking after, and looking for Pop, on many occasions in the intervening year and it seemed a good opportunity for us all to be together and would spread the burden of having to watch Pop all of the time.

We had happy times on the sands at Pendine when Pop would play cricket and have a paddle in the sea at high tide with the youngsters. In the evenings some of us would take Pop for his constitutional drink at a seaside hostelry before sun-down and after the children were in bed and being watched over by their mothers.

A memorable afternoon was enjoyed at a farm near in Pembrokeshire. This was owned by Freda and her husband, the sister of our deacon Philip and could only be accessed via a single track road, several miles long with grass in the middle and crossing through more than one ford. Really beautiful secluded rural countryside.

On our arrival Freda was sitting in an open barn, shucking peas into a large barrel. She asked for volunteers to help finish the job before tea would be served. Pop with some of the children finished the task expeditiously spurred on by the thought of something to eat and drink. A sumptuous feast of farmhouse produce with real cream was enjoyed by all and washed down with copious amounts of tea or homemade lemonade.

The last holiday that we took with Pop was in 1984, after our move to Sussex. We hired a Camping Coach on the North York Moors Railway at Goathland, when our two youngest, Jeremy and Bethany, were five and three years old respectively.

As a keen railway enthusiast, I determined that, while we were in Yorkshire, we would travel on the Settle to Carlisle line, then under threat of closure. There were only two trains each way at that time and so we set out, as early as we thought necessary, towards Settle. The roads across the moors were not nearly as fast as one is used to in the south and we were quite delayed finding it difficult to arrive on time.

In fact we spotted the train long before we arrived at Settle station. I parked as speedily as possible in the station car park after the train had already pulled into the station. Iris and the children made their way across the track and held open a door to wait until Pop and I caught them up. In their hurry, Bethany dropped her cuddly doll onto the track.

Pop insisted in retrieving the doll for Bethany and stooped down right behind the waiting train without any thought for his own safety or of any likelihood of another train going south. Pop and I boarded the train safely but breathless and without tickets!

The guard issued us a pass, with a telling-off for making the train late, but we had our ride to Carlisle. Thankfully, this beautiful line has now been saved as a working rail link to Scotland and the historic structures like Blea Moor tunnel and the Ribblehead Viaduct are still in use with now more than two trains per day!

During 1985, Pop started being regularly cared for in an old persons home in Hailsham. It was decided to repeat our holiday on the North York Moors Railway without him. He was not far from our thoughts, however, as on the day that we visited Scarborough, standing near to a chair lift, Iris and I looked at each other, hardly believing our ears. There was that jangling of Pop's pocket money, with which we had become so used, clearly audible to us both. After a split second we realised that the noise was emanating from the wheels of the chair-lift, not quite so silently as we had thought.

It was a haunting moment.

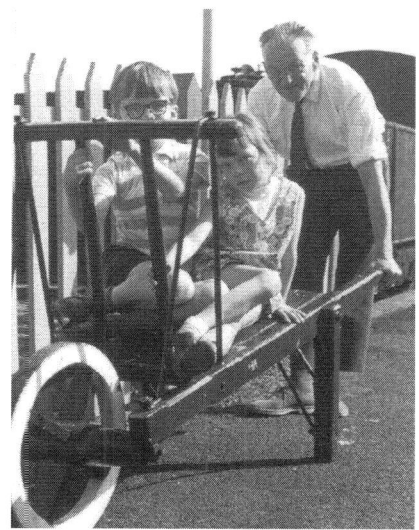

A happy day on the Severn Valley Railway

15 On the Bandwagon

Cousin John married Jennifer in Brighton on 7th July 1974 and we were invited as a family. All, that is, except Pop. What could he do when the day arrived?

Our friend John was to be involved with a carnival float for Hospital Radio Medway on the same day and agreed that Pop could assist! Surprised onlookers watched as "The Island Prince", an early small Showman's traction engine, puffed into Military Road, Chatham, pulling a cart with a bed, complete with patient, music emitting from a loudspeaker at each corner and an obvious earpiece fitted to the head of the "patient", leg in traction, supping ale from a bottle with a crate visible underneath adjacent to the inevitable bedpan. The flags fluttered as Pop laughed his way around town.

On Pop's birthday, 14th November 1974, Eric and Grace, landlord and landlady at the First and Last, Burham, had made him a cake. Iris and I were both indisposed that week and were unable to accompany him so the determined man made his own way to the furthest pub in the village from home. I phoned Eric to ensure that if he overstayed his welcome Pop would be brought home safely. Eric duly delivered him with a whole uncut cake, after closing time!

The regulars were disappointed but Pop had insisted that Iris would cut it later! "She's my guardian angel" he explained. The cake was eventually cut for a chapel tea held on the following Saturday. Iris had been unable to bake one herself because she had been in bed with influenza. We saw this as another provision from God, watching over us at this time.

Pop let us know his inner thoughts on an hourly basis with his constant muttering. We became quite used to him telling us we were in his thoughts when he would say under his breath, "miserable lot", usually when he had not got his own way. Alternatively, "nothin' ere; should have carried on", when he became impatient.

Then there was the occasion when John's stepmother was to move house in Sherborne and Pop and I went with Steve to assist the packing and house clearing. Pop was anxious to help, especially after a promise of a visit to the pub for a bite at lunchtime. We set him the task of clearing the coal store which at first he adapted to well.

Wielding a shovel and filling clean sacks with hard fuel lasted a while until he was down to the nutty slack. Wiping his face with a black sleeve he was heard to say "Joe Gormley wouldn't have it". He was clearly aware of the name of the then leader of the Mineworkers Union! We kept him occupied on this occasion and happily there were no attempts to "carry on".

16 *Silence in Church*

||||||||||||||||||||||||||||||||||||||||||||||||||||||||||||||||||||||||||||||||||||||||||||||||||||||||||

One evening we travelled with Pop to Sittingbourne, to the home of a deacon from the chapel. Philip suggested that we should each relate an answer to prayer or a word of testimony to God's glory, if we were able. I thought that Pop would have nothing to contribute except his incessant mumblings and his impatience before getting another drink. How wrong can one be!

Around the circle of those gathered, two spoke of their recent experiences and others stayed silent. Surprise took hold of us all when Pop stood up and lucidly explained that he had seen Jesus! "It was like this", he went on. "When I was in India I went for a walk one evening and got lost in the desert. I was very afraid and so knelt down and prayed to be led back to the camp. It was dark. When I looked up there was an apparition glowing white, right in front of me! It said 'It is I, be not afraid.', It was Jesus and He said 'follow me'. I followed Him a long way until we were on the path near the camp. Then He disappeared.

"That's when I saw Jesus."

Then there followed a stunned silence until the cups of tea came round. Pop came unhesitatingly to our chapel services each Sunday morning. He would sometimes mutter audibly before the opening hymn but would remain quiet during the remainder of the service.

One particular morning he sat next to me on the outside of the pew. I did not hear that squeaky door open whilst prayers were offered but on lifting my head the seat adjacent was empty. Pop had gone again! I slipped out of the building and peered up and down the street. No sign of Pop. The pub up the road had just opened its doors and as I had expected there in the nearest bar stood the erstwhile vagrant, pint in hand, smiling broadly as I approached. To my shame I lost my temper in self-righteous indignation, grabbed at the glass of beer, spilling the contents onto the floorboards and, taking hold of my father, marched him back into church.

We still had a lot to learn.

Pop with Mark and Beverley about this time

17 *Maidstone*

IIIIIIIIIIIIIIIIIIIIIIIIIIIIIIIIIIIIIIIIIIIIIIIIIIIIIIIIIIIIIIIIIIIIIIIIIIIIIIIIIIIIIIIIIIIIIIIIIIIIIIIIIIIIIIIIIII

Pop would never walk beside us when we were out and Iris and I discovered the reason. One day after we parted to do some shopping in different locations. I turned around to see Pop walking as usual, four feet behind Iris. Every few steps he would stoop down, almost surreptitiously, and pick up a dog-end from the pavement. This supplemented his weekly tobacco ration!

Once a week I took Pop into Maidstone to collect the unemployment benefit he now received. One particular morning the weather was chilly and a strong breeze blew up Gabriel's Hill as we came to the corner of King Street. I looked behind me before crossing the road.

Pop, holding onto the wall, became stiff and ghastly white and started to tremble from head to foot with fear. His teeth were chattering and his hand went up to his face. I put my arm around to steady him and for a moment thought he was having a fit. "It's the bodies" he said, "They haven't burned the bodies; it's the bodies". Pop was reliving some distant memory from the war as he smelled the odours from the pie shop drifting up the hill and mingling with the dust, petrol and diesel fumes!

Pop was of course very familiar with Maidstone from his childhood and youth. This we thought would be an advantage when in town as he would feel at home there. It

did, however, have the disadvantage that he knew some of
the corners and back-alleys with which I was not so familiar
and he was always on the look-out for a quick get-away. We
always had to be alert to his whereabouts and this was very
wearing on our nerves at times.

Collecting his money each week was something he looked
forward to with nervous anticipation. On one occasion a
queue had developed at the Labour Exchange and a rather
stout lady joined us to await her turn. She objected to Pop's
impatient mumblings and was quick to tell him so! It took a
lot of diplomacy to separate the two and preserve the peace!

The following week "Mrs Bigboddie" walked around
the people gathered, shouting "There he is!" To my relief
"Kenneth Sampson" was soon called and the tension was
broken as he walked away, money in hand, smiling in
anticipation of buying some more tobacco and having his
next drink.

The Old House at Home in Pudding Lane was a respectable
town pub and one pay-day Mother came with us to shop
while I took Pop to collect his money. We arranged to meet
later at this pub for a coffee and not surprisingly Pop and
I were first to arrive. Mother arrived a few minutes later
and I took the opportunity to leave them together whilst I
went to purchase a few more things. Upon my return I could
not see my Father. Mother was sitting near the door with a
face like thunder underneath her blue hat, without a drink.
This was a new experience for her. As I spoke to mother the
barman shouted to me: "You can take her out as well". It
was clear there had been an altercation. Pop's impatience to
have a drink had spilled over whilst waiting to be served and
leaning over the bar he had called out, "What d'ya think I'm

'ere for? Me 'ealth? " We were told in no uncertain terms that we would not be served there again.

We tried some occupational therapy during the evenings in the hope of keeping Pop's mind on something other than visiting the pub. Firstly there were the life drawing classes held in the local school. This went well initially and Pop would come home mumbling, "She's got bristols" after attempting to sketch a well-endowed lady. He soon tired of this activity, however, when the model was changed for a vase of flowers!

Sometimes Pop would play Scrabble or draughts with Mark and would also read to the children as they went to bed. He was always well behaved when in their company and they became quite fond of him despite his annoying and disruptive habits. One evening while I was away, Iris left him reading quietly downstairs while putting the children to bed. Suddenly she heard the noise, downstairs, of a door being closed. Pop had gone out. Iris had then had no choice but to continue her loving care of the little ones, then five and seven years old. In the meantime Pop returned, urinated on the kitchen floor and then retraced his steps to the Fleur-de-Lys, the nearest pub to our home. You can imagine Iris's fury and her dilemma as she anxiously sought to retrieve him.

She obtained help from our immediate neighbours to keep an eye on the sleepless children while she visited that pub and found his smiling face reflected in a beer glass.

Soon both back home to play Happy Families!

18 *The One That Got Away*

Remaining continually on our guard so that Pop did not give us the slip and disappear again, was a constant feature of our daily life and became quite a strain. However, opportunities for some respite did arise from time to time. John had a friend who sometimes took a fishing party on his boat in the Medway estuary and I hit on the idea of taking Pop with us.

After all, he could not run away whilst afloat and we would enjoy the bracing sea air together, especially as we were accompanied by men who would befriend him and thus enable him to share in our angling. The crate of beer stowed on board was an added attraction! We spent a long summer's day fishing, starting soon after first light, sailing downstream past Sheppey and out to sea until Reculver Towers came into view. We caught a few crabs some codling and a plaice. Pop enjoyed himself from the safety of the vessel and sometimes raised a laugh with his quips.

Feeling like old salts we made our return navigation in daylight towards Gillingham pier, the prevailing westerly wind quickly turning our pale faces into a ruddier hue, only to find on arrival that the tide was unfavourable for our usual disembarkation and mooring. Brian, our experienced boatman, therefore, decided to put down everyone except one other man at the end of the jetty. As I was sitting in the bow I remained on board to assist Brian in berthing the boat whilst the others walked the length of the pier to rejoin us.

The boat now made fast, Brian and I climbed across two other vessels alongside and climbed the rusting and barnacle-covered vertical ladder to the pier deck far above our heads. Our fellow fishermen had by now reached the place of our arrival. All, that is, except Pop.

"Where's the Old Man?" I asked John,

"Why, he was here with us a minute ago."

Quickly looking up and down the length of the pier I spotted him, some hundreds of yards away, climbing into the back seat of a car just as it was about to move from the pier head onto the road. I frantically waved my arms until the brake lights went on and the car stopped. "Where do you think you are taking him?" I asked the driver, breathlessly. "He's asked for a lift to the station," was the reply. Pop climbed out of the car shamefacedly. Once more, in the nick of time, I had been able to prevent my father from returning to vagrancy.

19 *On The Road*

During the three years Pop spent at Burham he gradually became more coherent and it was sometimes possible to hold short conversations. His attention span was short so we resorted to quick question and answer sessions to which we thought he would respond. The children were interested to know what their Grandad had been doing for the past twenty eight years whilst "on the road".

"What did you do when it rained, Grandad?" "Well, you would go into a wood and stand very still; the rain comes straight down all around you and you don't get wet", he replied.

He told us of a time when he walked across Romney Marsh and the rain was coming sideways. "I got wet alright then", he added. We could imagine his dishevelled figure closely holding his button-less coat around him, dripping wet and looking furtively for cover.

When travelling by car, Pop would look out for barns and "rate" them according to how comfortable they looked. The Dutch hay barns that were not full always appeared to be comfortable to him, and he told us that he used to lay up, keep warm and make himself invisible for a few days. "That was alright if there were no dogs about", he told us.

Food had never seemed to be a priority for him in those days although he was always hungry. His slight thin, bent figure belied the fact. When opportunities arose he would knock on the door of a country cottage or farmhouse and beg some cheese and bread. Sometimes he was given eggs or other types of food.

When met with a rebuff he just went on undeterred and still hungry, sometimes pulling root vegetables from a neighbouring garden or picking fruit from an orchard. He used an old tin can to boil water over a very small open fire that he had become adept at kindling and, if it was to be a feast, if he had any cocoa and sugar, he would stir some in and perhaps boil an egg.

On very cold days he could possibly be found in the corner of a public bar at a village pub. Sitting quietly, he would look furtively around quickly placing a nearly empty glass in front of him hoping that he would be less obtrusive and that the landlord would not notice him with his muddy feet firmly under a table. He still felt vulnerable.

He would search the ash-trays for long dog ends with which to make a roll-up and ask for a light hoping to become a member of the clientele. Hopefully someone would buy him a drink to refill his now empty glass. He might just be fortunate enough to spot someone's left-overs, maybe a partly eaten sandwich which he would quickly devour.

There were times when Pop had been given some casual labour. He was once a "sandwich-board" man in Sheffield, carrying a slogan for a local store as he wandered around the city. We wondered if it was he to whom our friends who lived there were referring when they said that their local "sandwich-board" man had disappeared from the streets recently! On other occasions he may have been found employment picking apples at harvest time. We knew, however, that these spells of casual employment would have been short-lived. Pop was really a town tramp and he walked in the country only to get from one place to another, if there was no suitable train. Train?

"So you travelled by train, Pop?" " Oh yes", he replied. "Took the Royal Scot once". "What about your ticket then?" we asked. "Well, you wait until the ticket collector comes along and then hurry to the toilet," he replied. "Got put off at Preston once," he explained.

When asked by the railway police where he was going, he said, "London", but they thought otherwise and he spent the night in a police cell, and he was given breakfast before catching the first train to Euston the following morning! Well, time did not really matter, did it?

"A lady magistrate once took pity on me," he said. "Poor man, you must have sore feet walking all around our country. Give him a pound from the Poor Box" The gavel came down. "Case Dismissed."

In London, Pop had a favourite hideaway. It was in a basement boiler house beneath a block of flats in St. John's Wood. He would never disclose exactly where this was, I don't know if this was because he was ashamed of the squalor that he lived in there or whether he thought that some day he might return. It was from here that he walked what became "his pitch" up and down Finchley Road, muttering to the flower seller at Swiss Cottage and befriending an old lady tramp too.

Loneliness set in near Christmas time and more than once he took a brick and threw it through a shop window a day or two before Christmas Eve. This would result in him spending Christmas in police custody, which was just what he wanted, of course.

Pop also remembered an occasion when he got locked in a garage overnight. He spotted two cars parked in a large open shed and whilst no one was to be seen, he opened the rear door of the largest and put his head down on the back seat. It was not long before he was fast asleep. It was dark when he awoke and there were two large metal doors, firmly barred from the outside.

"Were you found the next day?" we asked.

"No, it was Sunday and I thought I must stay for the weekend."

"What did you do then?"

"Well, I put some furniture on top of the car and climbed out through a roof light."

One winter's evening Pop was walking down Seven Sisters Road when a car screamed to a halt opposite. Men jumped out, smashed a window and grabbed as much jewellery as they could manage, got back into the car and sped away. Pop stood on the pavement opposite looking, until the police arrived.

"Did you see anything?" they asked. "They went down the road that way," he said, pointing in the opposite direction to where they had gone.

"Why did you do that Pop?" "Well, you never help the Police do you!" he retorted.

"They might lock you up." Simplicity at its best!

On another occasion Pop disappeared yet again and efforts to find him failed. We left it or a few days before I could make the journey to London to renew my search for him. As I sat in my office in Maidstone the phone rang and it was Iris. She had just received a call from the Swiss Cottage flower seller to say that he had seen the old tramp again. Iris's heart sank as she had quickly become used to the freedom that came with not having to watch Pop's every move.

Should she tell me or would it be better for us all to let him go this time? No, she could not do that now as a still small voice clearly said to her.

"He is a chosen vessel unto me."

(Acts 9:15)

The Holy Spirit at work!

Needless to say, I went up to Swiss Cottage that evening, and retrieved Pop once more.

In concluding this chapter of our life with Pop in Kent it would be remiss not to pay tribute to the people of Burham, particularly the landlords of each of the five public houses in the village at that time. They each accepted him and would "play the game" by looking after this man even at times when he was a nuisance and penniless.

The worshippers at Enon Chapel at Chatham had also taken Pop under their wings and have shared our concerns and griefs for Pop every time he disappeared.

Life moves on, however, and we needed to move to Sussex in 1975 due to my work commitments.

20 *Sussex*

I hurried back to my digs from the office at Hurstpierpoint. My friends had returned from holiday and following the usual warm greetings I was ushered into their front room.

"Your dad had a jolly good time," said Ned, holding aloft a near empty whisky bottle.

I lodged with a couple at their farm cottage near Albourne in West Sussex before finding suitable accommodation for my family in the vicinity. For two weeks in the summer whilst they were away on holiday, we all stayed there together, and my family enjoyed the locality whilst I was at work in Hurstpierpoint nearby.

Iris went to the sea-side at Brighton with the children and Pop on occasions and we joined up again for our evening meal in the cottage. Afterwards I would take Pop for a ride on the Downs, sometimes finishing up in a local hostelry. The day that my friend and his wife returned to their home I was greeted at the door. Having exchanged pleasantries about our mutual holidays I was asked to speak to the master of the house on his own. Advancing into his front room and having closed the door firmly behind us, he took a near-empty whisky bottle from behind the armchair.

"I see your Dad had a good time whilst we were away" he said, holding the bottle aloft so that the last vestige of pale brown liquid clung to the sides. "I guess Pop used to sit here when we were away," he smiled.

The light then dawned on me as to why Pop had been so happy to sit alone in the front room when we were there. We both had a chuckle over this incident. After a visit to an off-licence the status quo was restored.

Some may wonder how, as Christians, we were able to square our visits to pubs and the consumption of alcohol with a clear conscience. Firstly, I find no prohibition of alcoholic drink in the scriptures. Secondly I well remember the words of the minister with whom I lodged in Albourne.

"I have not so learned Christ."

My saviour was born in the stable of an inn two thousand years ago and I have wondered if this fact has ever exercised the minds of present day evangelicals.

The only suitable property available, having sold our Burham home, was a pretty, small, middle terraced cottage at Westmeston built from knapped flint. The situation was idyllic, snuggled under Ditchling Beacon, a high point of the South Downs, with the house in the Street leading to Westmeston Bostal, a well worn track leading directly up the escarpment to Ditchling Beacon. This location was only fifteen minutes by car to the office and within walking distance of the quaint village of Ditchling.

Pop thought it too remote to make unannounced excursions to a pub. We therefore settled to a routine that seemed to suit him. Chapel on Sundays at Henfield where we frequently stayed to dinner with the pastor and his family, regular shopping trips with Iris once a week to Burgess Hill or Hassocks, an evening trip into Henfield to a prayer meeting and visits to the secluded snug bar in the Bull at Ditchling afterwards, en-route for home.

We were lulled into a false sense of security as Pop would sleep during the afternoons at home and on an occasion of the Ditchling Fete we left him with the idea that we would return by six o'clock. However, we did not return until nearly seven only to find that Pop's bed was empty.

I made a speedy reconnoitre of the four pubs in Ditchling, and was informed by the licensee at the Sandrock that Pop had been in half an hour earlier but had left. Travelling around the lanes and nearby roads brought no better results. Perhaps Pop had hitched a lift but if so where should one look?

I went with Mark that evening as far as Godstone, looking inside every pub on the route but to no avail. It was now getting dark, so home we went in a distraught state of mind. Would I have to start all over again? I was exhausted and sobbed my heart out as I laid my head upon the pillow that night. It is amazing, however, how urgent, ardent prayer is answered from a sovereign God.

At 06:30 the following Sunday morning the phone rang. It was the police in Cambridge who advised us that they had arrested a man matching Father's description. Finding him sitting on a park bench, an observant WPC had asked him for his name. "Fred Smith," came the mumbled reply. "I do not think so, could it be Kenneth Sampson by some chance?" she asked. The game was up once more.

I was advised that he could not be detained for more than four hours, so could I collect him before ten? At 09:50 I was making my way into the police station in central Cambridge to find Pop once again, breakfasted and being given his personal effects such as they were before being released.

The slower journey home brought me to the understanding that constant vigilance is essential if one is to succeed in doing the will of God with regard to looking after someone like my father.

By the time we moved to Sussex, Pop had been with us for three years. What was his mental state after these years of reconciliation? He seemed to understand that he was with his family but still had the propensity to wander away to be on his own. This, we realised, was because he just could not accept responsibility, either for himself, or for others, and would walk away from the slightest inconvenience or disturbance or from any situation out of his regular routine.

He still mumbled the place names that were indelibly etched on his memory and repeatedly could be heard: "Harrow-on-the-Hill, Harrow-on-the-Hill", "Wolverhampton, Wolv'rampton, Middle Wallop, Middle Wallop, Arrowmanchis, Arrowmanchis, Swiss Cottage, Swiss Cottage, Finchley Road, Finchley Road," to name but a few.

There were, however, improvements in his concentration and by now Pop could hold short conversations before his mind wandered onto other things again. One thing was very noticeable: he responded to routine and regularity in all of our activities and any small degree of change would upset him. He also began to take an interest in his appearance and liked to be cleaner than before.

It was rather apposite that some time later, when Old Tom, a local vagrant, called at our home at Lower Dicker, Pop laughed and referred to him as "a dirty old tramp!" You could often tell Pop's whereabouts by the sound of the tinkling of money from within his pockets as he would constantly tap his trousers to make sure he was still solvent and so could not be accused of having "no visible means of support."

As a family we were by now more relaxed in dealing with this erstwhile tramp and most vestiges of our pride had been worn away through having had to deal with the most embarrassing and indelicate situations. Iris has often commented that a good sense of humour is a great blessing. Certainly, without being able to laugh at some of our experiences we could not have coped. Pop was gentle and kind to children and animals alike and frowned upon any degree of violence or unkindness.

Our friends in Henfield were able to look after Pop for a day each week to allow Iris some time to attend to the shopping alone and twice they offered to have him for a fortnight so that we could have a family holiday. Pop enjoyed having a beer in his room so that his wandering ways were minimised while we went to Scotland, camping by Loch Tummel.

Following Pop's decease we had a letter from our friends Graham and Renee from Henfield, describing the time that they looked after him whilst we were away. It read:

> *We knew something of the tense situations that arose for Pop's family; it was a joy to share a little of that burden. We knew our big house was given to us by God, for making it "open home" where there were needs. We always enjoyed Pop's weekly visits to us, and he won our affection. He needed as much watching as a small child because of his habit of wandering off.*
>
> *We were amused by the way he frequently muttered," disappear, disappear!", but it was our warning to keep a closer watch on him. One day he was sitting in the garden and our attention was briefly distracted from our look-out kitchen window. Suddenly we found*

*his seat had been vacated! Quickly Graham
was called from his study and he set off in hot
pursuit, in the direction of the pub.*

*Yes, Pop certainly was there, already half
way down a pint! We were left thinking he
had done a sprint over the 200 yards. Without
objection Pop returned to our home, though
not without murmuring of other intentions:
"Baker Street, Baker Street"*

*Our little boy of two or three was always a
close friend of Pop, sharing childrens' picture
books together. Pop's daily drink of beer was
often close at hand, and more than once he
offered the little boy a sniff. "lovely isn't it?
He would say. But mother was anxious that
the little boy would never become addicted to
the smell!*

*Whenever Pop was in our home we would
ask his help with drying up the dishes after
meals. With this task he would work at great
speed, resulting in the need for us to check
and re-dry on most occasions. But for the
person washing-up, the job must be done
very quickly to keep Pop occupied. Otherwise
he would never wait for items to land on the
draining-board, because as soon as it was
empty, Pop's tea-cloth would be put down
and he would return to his chair without
finishing the task.*

*Sometimes he would go with Graham for a
drive when visits were to be made.
Pop amazed us by his accurate knowledge
of places and names, even over wide areas
of the country. On one of these drives to*

Brighton, weaving the route through narrow
back-lanes in the town before Graham
eventually came towards a road junction.
"Guess you don't know where you are now,
Pop?"
There was an immediate response: "Yes!
Seven Dials", and he was quite right!

A new vicar was to be inducted at Henfield Parish Church later that year and our small congregation went to support the new incumbent. The parish church was packed as the impressive service began when the large oak doors were knocked upon by the Bishop's mace.

The voluminous building was filled with the singing of rousing hymns by the packed congregation. Pop had become separated from the rest of us but was held firmly in position by the crush. That is, until the communion wine was being offered to the faithful adherents of the Established Church. That was too much for him.

To my amazement I saw his familiar figure stepping across the seated congregation from pew to pew until he reached the altar rail! As the crowd dispersed after the induction service we were faced with the problem of locating Pop again but it took only a short while before we realised that the obvious place to start with was the Gardeners Arms where, sure enough, Pop was to be found again smiling behind a half empty pint glass.

During this period I was a scout leader with the 1st Ditchling Troop and we encouraged families to join in the annual camps. One year we went to the Lake District and camped near Watendlath. Pop came with Iris and I when Mark was a scout. There was also another husband and wife with us and Pop found it difficult to keep his eyes from following Lucy, a young mother, as she played rounders in shorts and a tee shirt. *"Thou must not covet"* he was heard to mumble, as he watched her ample breasts unmistakeably rising and falling under her thin shirt.

One day when I was away on a long hike across the fells with the Venture Scouts the remainder of the camp decided to go to Lake Windermere for a day. Pop was missing as they disembarked from the steamer at the quayside. Lucy's husband Peter with Iris made a speedy search of the area. Pop was found sitting on a bench eating an ice cream, just in time to make the return journey.

Pop enjoyed the Ditchling Royal British Legion ex-servicemen's suppers as well as the Remembrance Day parades when he would march proudly behind some rather more senior comrades. There was a Vice-Admiral, a Brigadier and a Colonel amongst the commissioned ranks.

Pop, determined to make his mark as a true infantryman, was always in step and upright as they marched behind the Cadets' band to the war memorial to hear the bugler play the Last Post.

Summer 1978 saw us cruising in a narrow boat for a weeks holiday, hired from a company in Aston, near Birmingham, situated in the old industrial canal system. I found this fascinating and relaxing, as Pop could not wander whilst we were afloat. Mother came with us as a prelude to her moving into our home the following year. The first afternoon took us from near Gas Street Basin to Wolverhampton, where we moored close to the busy railway station for the night. The ladies cooked dinner while Mark and I settled Pop with a visit to a nearby pub for a refreshing pint of midland ale.

An early night was welcome and we were all fast asleep before long, despite the constant noise of trains rattling their way towards the north, not many yards away. I was awakened suddenly by mother's voice shouting, "Peter, there's someone on the roof." I thought that perhaps we were

being disturbed by late night revellers but, looking cautiously
through the window, I saw a pyjama-clad figure sitting on a
canalside bench slowly rolling a cigarette. It was Pop! He
had left the boat by the front door which was self-latching
and having closed the door behind him, could not get back
in again to reach his bed.

> *My Grandfather—*
> *He stands at the bar*
> *And mutters to his boots*
> *Of places from afar*
> *And many trodden routes*
> *A beer in his hand, a fag in his mouth*
> *He speaks of the land that's to the north and*
>   *the south*
> *And while you hear him speak,*
> *He tells you all of Leeds*
> *You know his mind is weak*
> *But you should hear his needs.*
> *He tells you of a place from hiking on*
>   *the ridge*
> *And how he played an ace-*
> *The Tower and London Bridge*
> *And if you fix your mind*
> *on somewhere south of Kent*
> *He leaves you far behind*
> *and talks of north of Trent.*

Mark

ORDINARY
MEMBER

THE ROYAL BRITISH LEGION
HEADQUARTERS
49 PALL MALL,
LONDON, SW1Y 5JY

THIS IS TO CERTIFY THAT

KENNETH EWART SAMPSON

IS AN ORDINARY MEMBER OF THE

Ditchling

BRANCH OF THE ROYAL BRITISH LEGION

Member's Address Cloan Cottage

Westmeston

Hassocks

Badge No. ....

Date of joining ....23.7.7t.........

ENTRANCE FEE, 5p PAID

*Signature of Member...................................

*—It is essential that the member should sign here
in the presence of the Branch Secretary, and official fee
stamp receipt inserted covering the period of subscription.

21 The Dicker

During the early part of 1979 a telephone call from my mother determined that we should look for a larger home as she was about to lose the home that she had shared with her adopted son Michael for the past few years, as he was to remarry.

No, I insisted, I would not allow her to finish her days in an old peoples' home and determined that she would be given a home with us. Mother was sixty-four years old at that time. Our present house was too small for the needs of the five of us currently living there and so I started the search for larger accommodation. We also found that we were soon to become parents again!

The estate agent at Ditchling advised me to find a new home before putting Croome Cottage on the market. She was right. After several weeks of looking for a suitable property and having secured Old Mill Cottage a buyer was found for our Westmeston home within hours of placing it for sale.

Our new acquisition was in a dilapidated state and clearly needed months of work before it could be inhabited. Most remarkably, it transpired that the purchaser for our Westmeston home lived in Devon but knew the property as her son-in-law lived nearby at Streat where she had stayed on an annexe at his farm and had been friendly with the immediate past owner of our Croome Cottage.

Understanding that we needed time to repair our new home at The Dicker, the lady kindly offered us the benefit of a three month delayed contract so that there would be time to carry out essential building works in order to make the place habitable.

We knew this to be an amazing provision from God, as in answer to prayer, we were blessed with the words of the Fifth Commandment,

"that thy days may be long upon the land that the Lord thy God giveth thee."

(Exodus 20:12)

During July 1979 we moved, for the last time, into an old five bed-roomed house set in two and a half acres off The Dicker, near Hailsham in the countryside between Chiddingly and Hellingly. This house soon became home for the six of us, now including Mother who, although living under the same roof, needed separate accommodation from Pop! We also found room on our land for goats and geese and a little later on for a horse as well! Plenty of work was available here for any willing hands.

Pop was always happy to assist with any outside jobs that needed to be tackled. There was an occasion one winter when the doors to the goat sheds that I had built were unable to be opened because of ice forming at the base. Pop said to Iris " You should put hay under the doors, that will make it easier for them to open," a tip he had learned whilst in Canada. It worked!

And so a new chapter in our lives began.

There is a photograph of Pop in the kitchen of our new home, in its original state. At that time we were visiting The Dicker regularly to carry out some of the needful works in between the builders' visits and one can clearly see the dilapidated state of the place during this period.

We managed to keep Pop gainfully employed with the various chores as we cleaned up and prepared to move in. Pop generally joined in the activities of the day each time we visited and we always found him some useful job to do. Gardening was probably his favourite pastime as he was able to roll a cigarette and have a quiet smoke.

When he became bored he would say, "Shouldn't have come here in the first place" and would make as if to go away, but stayed where he knew he was safe. We became quite used to this expression as time went on. A new roof, a bathroom, a floor for the annexe, central heating and running water as well as a re-wire were completed before we moved in during July of that year. Decoration and conversion of the old scullery into a dining room were high on the agenda of things to do after we established ourselves in the new abode. All this before Iris gave birth to Jeremy during October, only three months after our move.

1979 was quite a hectic year but it felt like home by the time we celebrated Christmas and appreciated the fire roaring in the inglenook where the colourful decorations and low lighting gave our new home the feel of an old-fashioned Christmas card.

Iris was of course taken up with her duties of being a mother again and the gap left in looking after Pop was ably filled by Mother who keenly undertook some of the household chores and enjoyed being a grandma again to our new baby, Jeremy.

As the days lengthened into springtime Pop began to develop itchy feet and wanderlust again. We tried to keep his attention towards home and developed a routine of visits to some of the local hostelries which were further apart than he had been used to in Burham. Notwithstanding there would inevitably be times when our guard was down and Pop seemed to wait for these moments to make a break for freedom.

There were at least six public houses within a short drive from home and gradually I introduced Pop to most of them but our favourite was the Yew Tree Inn at Chalvington where Coleridge and Rhett Coomber were joint landlords. There was a camaraderie there and we met some interesting characters including Clarissa Dickson-Wright, with whom we shared a drink or two before she became a reformed alcoholic. The last time I met her was one lunchtime having a pint of orange juice and she told me how she had enjoyed listening to Pop as he became lucid after a drink or two.

There was a memorable occasion when, one evening, as it was getting dark, Mark and I went with Pop to the Yew Tree for a late evening drink. At that time there were building works in progress to alter the front bar and replace the floor. There was a note pinned to the front door asking patrons to use the rear entrance and so we had to go round to the back door past the heaps of contractors' materials and a mound of sand. Mark and I arrived inside and we ordered three pints.

"But there's only two of you," said Rhett.

"Pop is close behind," I replied.

After a pause the door opened and there from the gloom appeared Pop. He was covered from head to foot in sharp sand muttering "Cairo Cairo" with an outstretched arm ready to take his now much needed pint. The brick floor was soon covered with a dusting of sand while Pop clearly recalled his time in Egypt and the regulars had a good natured laugh.

We met a young man, Karl, with his girl-friend Anna at the Yew Tree and struck up a relationship with them. On one occasion, when Pop had gone away from home again, Karl met me in Hailsham and announced, "I saw your Dad the other evening, walking out of the May Garland," a pub near Horam, some five miles from home. I just wished that Karl had realised that Pop was off on his wanderings before he had had time to make his way to Sevenoaks.

A few days earlier we had a phone call from the police who advised that a man answering my father's description had been arrested at 06:00 hrs. that morning going from house to house collecting money from homes in a very respectable and quiet neighbourhood.

He said it was for the War Disabled, offering his Royal British Legion Membership card as identification. The sergeant on duty said that if I could be there before 09:00 hrs there would be no charges proffered as Sevenoaks is usually a quiet place at that time of day and Pop could keep the cash that he had on him at the time of arrest! I waited patiently as Pop was given back his belt, shoe laces, cigarettes, Royal British Legion Card, and sundry pocket paraphernalia as well as his small change from the charge sergeant that morning.

I always had mixed emotions when finding Pop under these circumstances-relief that he was safe and well, but anger because he had wandered so far from the place where he was wanted and loved. I was thankful too that the police usually saw sense in his release and returning him to where he would be looked after and perhaps learn to fend for himself.

22 *Married Again!*

Many times mother had expressed her revulsion against living with a retired tramp. I had frequently said that if she was to go to glory, she would have to honour her marriage vows which I reminded her included the words: "for richer, for poorer, in sickness and in health", so she must honour her husband, "until death do us part".

On one misty November evening I returned from work, not to be met by Iris with her usual friendly kiss at the door, but by mother. She said that she needed to have a private word with me. I wondered if she had had a disagreement with Iris or even if she wanted to move home, away from the sometimes difficult situations that inevitably occurred from time to time with Ken.

I suggested that we should have dinner first and then perhaps go for a ride in the car where we could be alone. She agreed, and after a quiet meal time we went out. Iris seemed to understand. I pulled up in a farm gateway, not so far from home. It was dark. The air was cold but still and the drips from the overhanging trees drummed loudly on the roof. Mother had not said a word. "What is the problem? What do you want to say". I asked.

111

Hesitantly, mother spoke: "I just want to go back with Ken," she said.

"What do you mean?" I asked.

"Well, I just want to be his wife again"

"Do you mean that you want to sleep with him?" I asked, only half believing what I had just heard. "Yes, that's it," she replied. The term "Gobsmacked" took on a new meaning for me from that moment and I was speechless for a time.

To say that I could hardly believe the situation is an understatement as I had never seen my parents together in union before. As we drove home, I think the only thing I said was that I would have to find them a double bed. How God goes ahead of you was clearly demonstrated by an event the next day at the office.

A colleague announced that friends of his were shortly moving house and had a settee that converted into a double bed which had become surplus to requirements. His friend would give it away if someone in need could transport it! Two evenings later I saw my mother and father together in the same bed for the first time in my life!

It was not all sweetness and light thereafter but mother did take her role as a wife more seriously, even to the point that she would bath my dad and ensure that he was clean and shaven each day. One morning shortly after, Pop was heard to mumble, "bin wi' me wife, bin wi' me wife, intercourse, intercourse". I was happy at that!

Two years of "married bliss" followed and Pop settled down to family routine for a time. This allowed Iris and I, along with our family, to have time apart without always having to looking over our shoulders to ensure that Pop was still with us.

Our daughter Bethany was born just after Christmas 1981. A family holiday was arranged, with a narrow boat, on the Midland canals during 1982 following a successful trip, the preceding year, with some Venture Scouts. We arrived in the middle of the afternoon, that day in May, at Midddlewich, to join Mark and two friends who joined our family on the ten-berth narrow boat "Maple".

They had arrived earlier in the day and had already stowed the provisions for the week. Our journey had taken longer than planned because mother had felt unwell and we had had to make some unscheduled stops. Mother had been diagnosed as having secondary tumours from her breast cancer some six years earlier and was due to go into hospital again for investigations into a possible brain tumour, on our return. What the diagnosis would be we had no doubt when we stopped en-route at one location and she walked into a door instead of opening it.

She had remarked earlier that her eyesight was becoming poor and the countryside had become a green blur as we travelled.. Whilst she appeared to be going blind, Pop was kind, helping her unsteadily onto the boat along a scaffold plank, after we first arrived, and she remarked that she would never be able to get off again!

The evening sun was beautiful as we made our way through the first set of locks to join the short Wardle Canal arm that leads to the Shropshire Union Canal at Barbridge Junction.

As we cruised leisurely I saw from the helm, in the waters of the canal, the green and black hull of the boat with red, yellow and blue motifs being distorted by the bow-wave as we leisurely cruised in the early evening sunshine. How beautiful was the Cheshire countryside with the many shades of the greens of late springtime. We decided to moor on the top of an embankment above Church Minsull where there is a view of the countryside around. The church bells below us were being rung that evening in preparedness for Sunday.

Mother sat on the forward deck enjoying the evening sun. She commented on the lovely sounds from the birds and the bells, and even if she could not admire the view, she enjoyed the experience, while Iris prepared our meals and Pop helped with the chores. Thus Mother passed, what proved to be the last few hours of her life, very happily with her family on a peaceful evening of our last holiday together.

Following dinner we cruised further along this arm of the cut and moored some quarter of a mile from the canal junction amongst some other colourful narrow boats as lamps were being lit within. After dark Mark, David, Graham and I took Pop to the Barbridge Inn on the junction before returning to rest after a busy and tiring day and we retired to our beds happily. Mother and Iris were already in their bunks.

The following day is one that will never be forgotten. I was awoken by a shout from one of the teenagers: "We can't get the door to the loo open. Someone's on the floor." It was mother; her face was blue and her body cold. I could feel no pulse.

"Leave her where she is and call an ambulance," I gabbled.

Three of us ran along the towpath as mist was rising over the cut. We scrambled down the embankment onto the nearest stretch of road and waved down a passing motorist, asking where the nearest public phone box is. These were the days before mobile phones.

A police car was first to arrive and the officer came with us to the boat. I was asked to take the boat to the nearest point accessible to the canal by an ambulance. That was bridge No. 100, on the Shropshire Union Canal some half mile past the junction.

The manoeuvring of a sixty foot narrow boat in reverse from between others to the centre of the cut and into slow forward gear to take the vessel into position to navigate round the right-angled junction takes some skill at any time and it was only with great concentration that I was able to overcome my emotions in navigating this waterborne hearse to the waiting ambulance and to moor again in a position to allow the ambulance crew and police access to the boat.

Pop stood pale faced on the muddy towpath watching as his wife's body was carried unceremoniously from aboard "Maple" around the corner of the bridge and into the waiting ambulance. "The Lord gives and The Lord takes away," he said as I sat next to the policewoman and was escorted to Leighton Hospital, Crewe.

The police advised that there would need to be a post-mortem examination before I could obtain the necessary certification to allow mother's body to be laid to rest. The owners of the narrow boat made provision for us to moor in their boat yard at Middlewich from that Sunday afternoon until we were able to complete matters with the Coroner and arrange for undertakers to handle matters thereafter. Our family remained in Cheshire until the following day, living on the boat until we were able to return home.

To the glory of God, it must be recalled that the costs of returning Mother to her final resting place were defrayed to the very pound, through the gifts of kind friends, following much prayer over our concerns in this matter. Mother was laid to rest the following week at Zoar Chapel, The Dicker, Hellingly by the Pastor, Mr. J.W.Sperling -Tyler FRAS who had taken a keen interest in Pop since our arrival at Lower Dicker when we began as a family to attend Zoar Chapel.

This kindly gentleman had been brought up in the East End of London and was familiar with the plight of down-and-out characters from his youth. For his part Pop respected his Pastor, especially when he discovered that he was not teetotal and liked a drink of Guinness from time to time! There was one occasion, when visiting the Pastor's home to get some forms signed to give me Power of Attorney over Pops finances, when Pop hesitatingly asked, looking down at a nearby shopping basket, "Do you partake of a little bevvy, sir."

Pastor Sperling-Tyler replied, smiling, "Well, as a matter of fact I do".

This was toasted by the three of us with a shared can of Guinness to Pop's great delight. Pastor Sperling-Tyler confided to me that he was sure that Pop was one of God's chosen vessels "If it were not so you would not have had the Lord's blessings showered upon you in your desire to find and look after your father," he said with discernment.

23 *The Widower*

The owner of Middlewich Narrow Boats was a Christian, and allowed us to have another week on the canals, without charge, due to the curtailment of our earlier holiday on "Maple" during May 1982 and so we set off again to the Midlands later in the year when my Godson, Timothy, accompanied us. This time we navigated the Cheshire Ring.

We had a peaceful and enjoyable time afloat stopping off for a pint and a sandwich at a canal-side pub each day and Pop became thoughtful and quiet enjoying his pint whilst remembering the events of our previous canal trip.

Indeed, during the next three years Pop seemed to settle down to family life and became more lucid, occasionally talking about some of his travelling exploits. He enjoyed his daily social drink, usually at the Yew Tree, and gave us few problems.

He was interesting to be with as he occasionally described some of his travelling experiences to Mark or Beverley, who, in amusement would emulate some of his actions. But he was overheard to say softly on one occasion, words from one of William Cowper's hymns:

Can a woman's tender care
cease towards the child she bare,
Yes, she may forgetful be,
yet will I remember thee.

He would still mumble to himself audibly and we would often be aware of his thoughts which he just could not keep to himself.

"Better off elsewhere", or "should have kept going, rotten crowd."

When visiting a new location Pop would sometimes say "nothin' here-miserable lot".

A visit to Richmond to deliver Christmas presents to my brother Michael set off a chain of extraordinary events. Pop got up to use the toilet and as he walked across the long piled cream carpet a trail of liquid brown excrement followed him. The attempts to clean him up proved that he had very swollen legs from which we could scarcely remove his trousers.

A visit to the doctor the following day took him quickly by ambulance into St.Mary's Hospital Eastbourne, where he was admitted with suspected heart failure. The diagnosis was poor so we were determined that we should stay with Pop as long as practicable.

The physician in charge suggested that someone from the family should remain with him during that Christmas Eve night. Mark volunteered to stay with his Granddad, where he remained at his bedside, until the early hours of Christmas morning.

Our first concern on Christmas Day was for Pop. The whole family walked apprehensively past the ward where he was sleeping earlier and could see through the window that his bed was empty. With heavy hearts we approached the ward only to find it deserted. There was, however, the noise of laughter coming from the nearby dining room.

As we entered we saw Pop – paper hat on head – laughing as he enjoyed yet another community Christmas, sitting between two elderly ladies and about to pull crackers! The best Christmas present that we could have had that year. And so life went on.

It wasn't long, however, that Pop began to develop worsening health problems and one day he closed the X-Ray Department at the District General Hospital in Eastbourne! I arrived home that morning, just having left Pop, under some duress, in the care of a well-meaning but brusque sister attending those sitting in the corridor-cum-waiting area. I had been in the dressing cubicle with Pop showing him how to tie-up his white gown behind, in readiness to have a barium-enema X-Ray. Pop was not happy!

I tried to explain to the sister that unless I remained with my father, she would have problems but she was adamant that she was well used to looking after all manner of patients and that Pop posed no particular difficulty for her! So I left Pop in her care.

The telephone was ringing as I drew up outside our home. It was an irate sister from the DGH saying, "come back quickly, Mr. Sampson. Your father is running around the hospital grounds with only his gown on!" In my mind I could hear him saying, "shouldn't have come here in the first place" as I drove towards the hospital for the second time that day.

By the time I arrived, Pop was back in the corridor, the red-faced sister overseeing him. She told me to get him dressed and to make another appointment. I refused in tones of constrained politeness and said that if my father was refused his X-Ray today, there was no way I could get him to come back again. "If it was really necessary an X-Ray would have to be done immediately," I insisted. This time she listened!

Having had a quiet word with the radiographer and having got me fitted with a lead-lined apron, I was ushered into the inner-sanctum. "Rotten crowd" Pop announced, as he was asked to kneel on the examination table. I stood aside trying to assure Pop that he would be all right if he would do as asked. I watched tensely as the white barium liquid was injected into his back passage. The radiographer adjusted the photographic equipment into its optimum position.

Without warning or request there was a loud rumbling as Pop released his pent-up flatulation with as much force as he could muster. The air in the room became laden with tiny droplets of a creamy-brown liquid which settled on the walls, ceiling and furniture as well as the persons standing by. "Shouldn't 'ave come 'ere in the first place" said Pop in a subdued tone.

Peering right into his face, the radiographer replied, "the feeling, my friend, is mutual, I assure you". X-Ray over, back in the changing cubicle, I helped Pop to dress. I was amused and somewhat satisfied to hear an embarrassed sister explaining to those still waiting that they would have to make another appointment, as the Department was to be closed for the day for deep-cleaning.

24 *End of the Road*

The telephone rang late one Saturday evening. "Is that a Mr. Sampson?" said the voice from afar. "I am searching for a David Sampson who served in the RAF during the second World War."

"I am afraid I do not know a David Sampson," I replied. "I did, however, have an Uncle by the name of Eric, who I know was in Bomber Command and who, I believe, was awarded the DFM for his services."

" Do you have a contact for him?"

" No. I do not have his present address, but I do know that he lived in the Southend area of Essex."

Clearly the person on the phone was anxious to make contact and advised that he was an aeronautical historian, researching some World War Two histories. I had known that his sister, my aunt Marjorie, had lived in Maidstone for some time and I remembered that her last address was at Wolfe Road. Nothing was to be lost, so I telephoned her to ask Eric's address. She was not very forthcoming, to say the least, and said that she would firstly contact Eric to find out if he would mind her divulging his details!

Some weeks passed and I had had no response, so I phoned her again and with some reluctance she told me that she did not think Eric would be particularly pleased to hear from me. I did, however, elicit his phone number from her and straightaway telephoned my uncle. Having explained the reason for my call and telling him that I was his brother's son, Eric immediately said, "of course, Ken has been dead for some time now". I explained that Ken was here with me, alive and well. There was a prolonged silence.

I never found out if Eric spoke with the aeronautical historian who had precipitated this contact, but it little mattered as I now was able to contact him. It was with considerable satisfaction, therefore, that, on the morning of 10th November 1990 I saw Marjorie and Eric walking along the sea-front at Eastbourne.

By this time Pop was living in a care home in Hailsham and an eightieth birthday party was organised for him at Harebeating House, where he dwelt. Many people, including his brother and sister had been invited and Marjorie and Eric were on their way there when I spotted them!

Pop was reunited with his brother and sister later that day when we all had a good time. During his stay at Harebeating Pop was still occasionally prone to resume his old wandering habits. Our telephone rang at about 6am one Sunday morning in October. It was the local police who had found an elderly gentleman sitting on the kerb in the High Street, dressed only in shirtsleeves and trousers. The weather was cold and there was a ground frost.

Fortunately there was a name-tab at the rear of his clothing with "K.Sampson" clearly visible." Do you know anyone of this name?" the constable asked. Pop was soon returned to the home from which he had strayed, and when we visited him later, we found he was none the worse for his early morning walk. He had been out of routine as the clocks had "gone back" the previous night!

During the next two years Pop was transferred to Grangemead, Hawthylands Road, and was quite happy there. We would take him out for one day each week when he usually had a much welcomed trip to the Yew Tree, where his mumblings and gestures still kept the locals amused and his long arms would still reach to the bar for his pint.

During the spring of 1992, Pop contracted several chest infections and his general health gradually deteriorated but he was nursed with care and affection until he died peacefully in the early hours of 4th May. Having visited a nearby deacon from our chapel at The Dicker, to advise the church of father's death, Iris and I made our way to the Yew Tree to tell some of those who knew him.

Unexpectedly, we were greeted by some friends from Crowborough, John Burch and his wife who were having morning coffee. We were able to find solace in speaking with them and sharing God's goodness to us over so many years whilst we cared for Pop.

25 *Despised in Death*

When mother had been buried in the graveyard at Zoar Chapel, The Dicker, Hellingly we had purchased a double plot in which to lay to rest my father too at the appropriate time. Pop had consistently attended the services at Zoar whilst Iris and I were members there and it had been assumed that his burial service would be held in that chapel.

Pastor Sperling-Tyler had been deceased then for some time and there was as yet no incumbent Pastor. Since our erstwhile pastor, Leslie Jarvis, from Chatham, had been instrumental in finding Pop, we had no hesitation in requesting him to officiate. The deacon in charge of the burial ground thought otherwise, however, and Mr. Jarvis was refused permission to conduct the funeral service at Zoar!

We therefore had to hurriedly seek an alternative place for the service to be held and were charitably welcomed to Hailsham Baptist Church with only the interment at Zoar Chapel, where Father now rests alongside his wife and in the same burial-ground as the Pastor who nurtured him.

As if the refusal to allow our chosen pastor to officiate at the service was insufficient, the deacon, previously referred to, told the undertakers, in my hearing, that he would still make a charge for use of the premises at Zoar as the toilets would be open! I believe the poor man must have missed the real Gospel message despite many years of chapel attendance.

Pop's brother Eric and sister Marjorie attended the funeral with many other relations. One of James Montgomery's hymns which we sung that day seemed to sum up Pop's life:

> *"For ever with The Lord!"*
> *Amen, so let it be!*
> *Life from the dead is in that word*
> *'tis immortality*
> *Here in the body pent*
> *absent from Him I roam*
> *yet nightly pitch my moving tent*
> *a days march nearer home."*

After the funeral we met for a wake at our home and it was here that I first met my cousin Mike and we began to restore those silent years denied to us as children. It was at Mike and Hannes' home later where it transpired that Aunt Marjorie had still not told her son, my cousin Adrian, that he had had an uncle Ken. This was disclosed at a family reunion where Adrian asked me how I was connected to the family. His mother Marjorie very quickly jumped to her defence with the statement "well, all families have their black sheep".

Adrian was quite put out by this as I explained the circumstances surrounding my father, his uncle Ken, from an early age. Adrian and I have been good friends since that day, and upon his mother's decease, he bequeathed me an antique cabinet which had belonged to his parents and grandparents. This stands in our lounge to this day.

Mike, Adrian and I together with our respective families have subsequently remained in touch and as good friends. We, as three first cousins, who have led very different lives and experiences, nevertheless share a common ancestry through Grandfather John and Grandmother Maggie Sampson and can relate to each other without any sense of shame or embarrassment resulting from incidents in the distant past.

Epilogue

The course of my father's life has been run and we believe that he is now in Glory. Looking back, we would not have had our lives ordered in any other way and our family remember Pop with much affection, as do many who were acquainted with him. I was reminded of him the other day when someone quoted from Psalm 34 where we read,

"this poor man cried and the Lord heard him, and saved him out of all his troubles."

(Psalms 34:6)

Pop had quoted part of this verse many times, under his breath, when recalling the past. I believe this poor man possessed a firm faith underneath a broken frame. The effect of Pop's life upon our family was not inconsiderable. It necessitated me giving up my share in a business, moving home to find regular employment and later to move again to accommodate Mother and Father together under the same roof. In turn our children had had to change schooling which was more unsettling than we had anticipated.

Notwithstanding, every one of our family have said that it was the right thing to do. They have witnessed love in action in the face of adversity. The police were also able,

in those years, to exercise their own discernment in dealing with the human issues then at stake, unlike today, in an era when "tick-box" policing seems to be the norm to assist with controlling government statistics.

We also developed an understanding for those so much less fortunate than ourselves and particularly those suffering from the results of war, like "Old Tom", who mumbled his way around Dickerland for many years, always polite, but needing to be fed and watered.

Chiddingly churchyard holds Tom Jessop's grave with a simple headstone contributed by some of those in the locality who knew and helped him and became fond of him, another one from the road. Lessons of faith have been learned from some of the more difficult circumstances faced at the time.

It has become clear that not all understand that the priesthood of believers need to exercise their own conscience in communicating with Almighty God through the power of the Holy Spirit to the Lord Jesus Christ.